Tovim M[...]

A GLIMPSE OF LIGHT

Gems of Tanach

Written by
Reb Moshe Steinerman

Edited by Elise Teitelbaum

Ilovetorah Jewish Outreach Network

iloveTorah Jewish Publishing
First Published 2018
ISBN: 978-1-947706-00-2

Copyright: iloveTorah Jewish Publishing
www.iloveTorah.com
moshe@ilovetorah.com

ABOUT THE AUTHOR

Rabbi Moshe Steinerman grew up as a religious Jew on the hillsides of Maryland. During his teenage years, Reb Moshe developed his talent for photography, while connecting to nature and speaking to HaShem. He later found his path through Breslov *Chassidus*, while maintaining closeness to the *Litvish* style of learning. He studied in the Baltimore *yeshiva*, Ner Yisrael but then married and moved on to Lakewood, New Jersey. After settling down, he began to write Kavanos Halev, with the blessing of Rav Malkiel Kotler *Shlita*, *Rosh Yeshiva* of Beis Medresh Gevoah.

After establishing one of the first Jewish outreach websites ilovetorah.com in 1996, Reb Moshe's teachings became popular amongst all spectrums of Jews from those unaffiliated to ultra-Orthodox. His teachings grew popularity due to their ideals of drawing Jews together and his hundreds of stories of *tzaddikim*. Reb Moshe made *aliyah* to Tzfat in 2003 and returned over 20,000 English-speaking Jews to Judaism through his thousands of Jewish videos and audio *shiurim*. His learning experience includes the completion of both Talmud Bavli and Yerushalmi as well as other important works.

In 2012, Reb Moshe, with his wife and children, moved to Jerusalem. Some of his other books are Kavanos Halev (Meditations of the Heart), Tikkun Shechinah, Chassidus, Kabbalah & Meditation, Yom Leyom (Day by Day), Pesukei Torah (Passages of Torah), Pathways of the Righteous, Prayers of the Heart, A Journey into Holiness, and The True Intentions of the Baal Shem Tov. Thousands have read the advice contained in these books, with life changing results.

In Memory of my holy father R. Shlomo Zavel Ben Yaakov ZT"L
My father-in-law Menachem Ben Reuven ZT"L
Toba Esther Bas Gedalya Aharon HaKohein
And all the great souls of our people

Dedicated to my wife Rochel
and to my children Shlomo Nachman, Yaakov Yosef, Gedalya
Aharon Tzvi, Esther Rivka, Yeshiya Michel, Dovid Shmuel,
Eliyahu Yisrael
May it bring forth the light of your neshamos

Dear Reader,

Ilovetorah Jewish Outreach is a non-profit and books and Torah classes are available at low costs. Therefore, we appreciate your donation to help Rabbi Moshe Steinerman and ilovetorah.com to continue their work on behalf of the Jewish people. We also ask that you pass on these books to others once you are finished with them.

Thank you,
Reb Moshe Steinerman

www.ilovetorah.com
Donations: www.ilovetorah.com/donations

RABBINICAL APPROVAL / HASKAMAH

Dear Friends,

I have read the manuscript of "<u>A Glimpse of Light, Gems of Tanach</u>" by Reb Moshe Steinerman of Tzfat. Mr. Steinerman has taken eighteen topics and collected eighteen verses culled from Tanach dealing with each topic. His short and pithy comments on these verses serve as positive lessons and inspiration.

I have found the work compatible with true Torah outlook and *hashkafa* and a tool to strengthen one's appreciation of Torah's ideas and a motivation for drawing closer to service of HaShem.

May HaShem grant the author life and health to be able to continue to benefit the community in strengthening and enhancing Torah knowledge and observance.

Sincerely,
With Torah blessings

Rabbi Zev Leff

Approval from the Biala Rebbe of New York

הובא לפני גליונות בעניני קירוב רחוקים לקרב אחינו בני ישראל אל
אביהם שבשמים, כידוע מהבעש"ט זיע"א שאמר "איתמי קאתי מר
לכשיפוצו מעינותיך חוצה" ואפריון נמטי"ה להאי גברא יקירא מיקירי
צפת עיה"ק תובב"א כמע"כ מוהר"ר משה שטיינרמן שליט"א אשר כבר
עוסק רבות בשנים לקרב רחוקים לתורה וליהדות, וכעת מוציא לאור
ספר בשם "טובים מאורותי" וראיתי דברים נחמדים מאוד וניכר מתוך
הדברים שהרב בעל המחבר - אהבת השי"ת ואהבת התורה וישראל
בלבבו, ובטחוני כי הספר יביא תועלת גדולה לכל עם ישראל.

ויה"ר שיזכה לבוא לגומרה ברוב פאר והדר ונזכה לגאולתן של ישראל
בב"א.

בכבוד רב:
אהרן שלמה חיים אליעזר
בלאאו"ר שלמה"ה אב"ד

Rabbi M. Lebovits
Grand Rabbi of
Nikolsburg
53 Decatur Avenue
Spring Valley, N.Y. 10977

יוסף יחיאל מיכל
לעבאוויטש
ניקלשבורג
מאנסי - ספרינג וואלי, נ.י.

בעזהשי"ת

בשורותי אלו באתי להעיד על מעשה אומן, מופלא מופלג בהפלגת חכמים ונבונים,
ירא וחרד לדבר ח, ומשתוקק לקרב לבות ישראל לאביהם שבשמים,
ה"ה הרב **משה שטיינערמאן** שליט"א בעיה"ק צפת תובב"א

שעלה בידו להעלות על הספר דברים נפלאים שאסף מספרים הקדושים, בענין אהבה
אחוה שלום וריעות, לראות מעלות הברינו ולא חסרונם, ועי"ז להיות נמנעים מדברי
ריבות ומחלוקת, ולתקן עון שנאת חנם אשר בשביל זה נחרב בית מקדשינו
ותפארתינו, וכמשאחז"ל (רש"י. ובקרא רבה ט' ס) על ויזן שם ישראל, שנותנה תורה באופן
שחנו שם כאיש אחד בלב אחד.

וניכר בספר כי עמל ויגע הרבה להוציא מתח"י דבר נאה ומתוקן, ע"כ אף ידי תכון
עמו להוציא לאור עולם, ויהי רצון שהפיץ ה' בידו יצליח, יברך ה' חילו ופועל ידו
תרצה, שיברך על המוגמר להגדיל תורה ולהאדירה ולהפיצו בקרב ישראל, עד ביאת
גוא"צ בב"א

א"ד הכותב לכבוד התורה ומרביציה.
י"ט חשון תשס"ו

בס"ד

RABBI DOVID B. KAPLAN
RABBI OF WEST NEW YORK
5308 PALISADE AVENUE • WEST NEW YORK, NJ 07093
201-867-6859 • WESTNEWYORKSHUL@GMAIL.COM

דוד ברוך הלוי קאפלאן
רב ואב"ד דק"ק
וועסט ניו יארק

י' שבט ה'תשע"ז / February 6, 2017

Dear Friends,

Shalom and Blessings!

For approximately twenty years I have followed the works of Rabbi Moshe Steinerman, Shlit"a, a pioneer in the use of social media to encourage people and bring them closer to G-d.

Over the years Rabbi Steinerman has produced, and made public at no charge, hundreds of videos sharing his Torah wisdom, his holy stories, and his touching songs. Rabbi Steinerman has written a number of books, all promoting true Jewish Torah spirituality. Rabbi Steinerman's works have touched many thousands of Jews, and even spirituality-seeking non-Jews, from all walks of life and at all points of the globe.

Rabbi Steinerman is a tomim (pure-hearted one) in the most flattering sense of the word.

I give my full approbation and recommendation to all of Rabbi Steinerman's works.

I wish Rabbi Steinerman much success in all his endeavors.

May G-d bless Rabbi Moshe Steinerman, his wife, Rebbetzin Rochel Steinerman, and their beautiful children; and may G-d grant them health, success, and nachas!

With blessings,

Rabbi Dovid B. Kaplan

11

Rabbi Abraham Y. S. Friedman
161 Maple Avenue #C Spring Valley NY 10977
Tel: 845-425-5043 Fax: 845-425-8045

בעזהשי"ה

ישפות השם החיים והשלו', לכבוד ידידי מאז ומקדם מיקירי קרתא
דירושלים יראה שלם, זוכה ומזכה אחרים, להיות דבוק באלקינו, ה"ה
הר"ר משה שטיינרמאן שליט"א.

שמחתי מאוד לשמוע ממך, מאתר רחוק וקירוב הלבבות, בעסק
תורתך הקדושה ועבודתך בלי לאות, וכה יעזור ה' להלאה ביתר שאת
ויתר עז. והנה שלחת את הספר שלקטת בעניני דביקות בה', לקרב
לבבות בני ישראל לאבינו שבשמים בשפת אנגלית, אבל דא עקא
השפה לא ידענו, ע"כ לא זכיתי לקרותו, ע"כ א"א לי ליתן הסכמה פרטי
על ספרך, ובכלל קיבלתי על עצמי שלא ליתן הסכמות, ובפרט כשאין
לי פנאי לקרות הספר מתחלתו עד סופו, אבל בכללות זכרתי לך חסד
נעוריך, היאך הי' המתיקות שלך בעבדות השם פה בעירינו, ובנועם
המדות, וחזקה על חבר שאינו מוציא מתחת ידו דבר שאינו מתוקן,
ובפרט שכל מגמתך להרבות כבוד שמים, שבודאי סייעתא דשמיא
ילווך כל ימיך לראות רב נחת מיוצ"ח ומפרי ידיך, שתתקבל הספר
בסבר פנים יפות אצל אחינו בני ישראל שמדברים בשפת האנגלית
שיתקרבו לאבינו שבשמים ולהדבק בו באמת כאות נפשך, ולהרבות
פעלים לתורה ועבודה וקדושה בדביקות עם מדות טובות, בנייחותא
נייחא בעליונים ונייחא בתחתונים עד ביאת גואל צדק בב"א.

כ"ד ידידך השמח בהצלחתך ובעבודתך

FOREWORD

With so many spiritual and practical books available to study, many have overlooked the greatness of *Tanach*. It contains many spiritual secrets and is the source of all Jewish law. To uncover and appreciate it has been the goal of sages for generations, since the giving of the Torah. Yet, the more these sages managed to uncover these gems of wisdom, the further they seemed from conquering it. It is stated, "Its measure is broader than the earth and wider than the sea" (Job 11:9, Psalms 119:96). Please realize that no single book could ever encompass the full knowledge of *Tanach*. My goals in the pages that follow is to glimpse her light and reopen some of the wisdom she contains.

Were it not for the great sages who came before us, the light of *Tanach* would be inaccessible. Our holy sages have enhanced our understanding of *Tanach* throughout Jewish history. By traveling these roads, the light of *Tanach* is revealed. It was the way of Rav Zusya of Hanipoli that, when he didn't understand something, he would go to a private room and cry until HaShem said, "Enough," and opened Rav Zusya's mind to the understanding he desired.

There were many instances when I too had no idea how to open the hidden light in a particular verse; it was during these moments that I cried out to HaShem and prayed for wisdom and enlightenment. Other times I just refused to leave my place until I understood the verse, and through this, I managed to open doors to a world I never knew existed.

* *

May it be HaShem's will that the light of the Torah be open before us in this crucial time before the final Redemption. I pray that this book will open your hearts and minds to new ideas – bringing you to answers that you never knew existed.

Thank you, HaShem, for all Your help in making this Torah writing project a reality.

Reb Moshe Steinerman

TABLE OF CONTENTS

Reb Moshe Steinerman

INTRODUCTION

The Hebrew word Tanach is the acronym *TaNaCh*, or תנך. These letters are from the three divisions of the Hebrew Bible: the Torah, Nevi'im, and Kesuvim. I used my knowledge of the Midrash, Talmud and Chassidic teachings to give my own *chidushim* for selected verses.

This book is written such that everyone, regardless of background, can see an opening of light in a world full of darkness. As our sages said, "A passage from scripture can yield many meanings, just as a hammer splits one rock into many fragments." (Sanhedrin 34a) Picking up some of these fragments has been a tremendous learning experience for me and has shown me how all wisdom stems from the light of Tanach.

In order to understand and internalize the Tanach, it is critical that you feel what you are reading. In your mind, take yourself back in time. Generations ago, even the simplest Jew read the Haggadah on *Pesach* and felt as if he was building bricks and suffering torture at the hand of the Egyptians. When he read about the Exodus from Egypt, he felt as if he was traveling in the desert with Pharaoh's army close behind.

Rav Kalonymus Kalmin once said, "When you learn Tanach, try to identify with all the happenings as if you yourself were there at the time. Go with Abraham and Isaac to the binding of Isaac on the altar; involve yourself in the anguish and fear of Jacob when he prayed to HaShem to save him from the wrath of his brother Esav." (Hachsharat ha-Abrechim, chapter 7, p.33)

17

To understand some of the verses, I had to mentally travel back in time. Other times, I had to travel into the future. I tried to understand how we, as a nation, would feel during a revelation of G-dliness. Little by little, I received an understanding, which I wish to give over to you.

CHAPTER 1: HAPPINESS

"You shall rejoice before HaShem, your HaShem."
(Deuteronomy 12:18)

Rejoice before HaShem! Don't be happy only when you see the good things He has given you; delight in HaShem just because He is your Creator. This is the greatest reason to rejoice.

"The heart of those who seek HaShem will rejoice." (Psalms 105:3)
Just knowing that you want to come close to HaShem should make you ecstatically happy. How many people even try to seek out the ways of Truth?

"I will rejoice with HaShem; my soul will be joyful with my HaShem." (Isaiah 61:10)
If you want to be happy, simply connect yourself to HaShem, blessed be He, and that attachment itself will bring you joy.

"I will rejoice at your word as one who finds great spoils." (Psalms 119:162)
The commandments are there as vehicles to bring us enlightenment and joy - that is if we value them.

"Serve HaShem with gladness; come before His presence with singing." (Psalms 100:2)

What makes a master take pleasure in His servant? When the servant does his work with pride and joy, seeking only to bring pleasure to his master.

"Serve HaShem with fear and rejoice when there is trembling." (Psalms 2:11)

When a person has a phobia, whether of an object or situation, it brings him sadness and discomfort. Fearing HaShem in the proper way brings rejoicing to one's soul.

"The precepts of HaShem are righteous, rejoicing the heart." (Psalms 19:9)

A person is sad when a negative thought enters his or her mind. If you think about doing *mitzvos* then positive thoughts should return, making you happy again.

"Because you did not serve HaShem, your HaShem, with joyfulness and with gladness, [you received punishment]." (Deuteronomy 28:47)

It's not a sin to be depressed. It is worse than committing a sin because it leads to idolatry and countless other sins.

"Light is sown for the righteous and joy for the upright in heart." (Psalms 97:11)

There is normal joy and there is a joy attained from doing the *mitzvos*. This joy is filled with light.

"A merry heart is good healing medicine." (Proverbs 17:22)

The majority of ailments people suffer come from a saddened heart. At the onset of any pain, immediately jump up with joy and give thanks to HaShem. You will notice an improvement in your health.

"All the days of the poor are evil, but he with a merry heart has a continual feast." (Proverb 15:15)

If a person is poverty-stricken and complains of his lot, he is sure to abandon his Creator out of spite. However, once he rejoices in what he does have, then every day will bring new hope and fill his soul like a feast.

"That I may come to the altar of HaShem; to HaShem, the gladness of my joy." (Psalms 43:4)

The greatest joy is when a person feels nullified in the will of HaShem; standing before His altar like a child before his father.

"Let my words be pleasant to Him; I will rejoice in HaShem." (Psalms 104:34)

There is a certain level of joy during which a person feels as if his lips are connected to the *Shechinah*. His words come forth as pleasant cries, full of sweetness and yearning. The words come from deep within, carrying with them the joy of the next world.

"Israel will be happy in its Maker. The sons of Zion will rejoice in their King." (Psalms 149:2)

If you are happy with HaShem and with what He gives you, HaShem will allow you into His palace where you will rejoice in spiritual bliss - the light of HaShem. We must be happy simply in HaShem.

"And the righteous will rejoice. They will exult before HaShem and be filled with happiness." (Psalms 68:4)

When a person is righteous in his ways, joy will certainly follow. If you find yourself saddened, make yourself exceedingly righteous. Even someone far from HaShem can return immediately to a righteous path; all you need is the desire to change.

"Let my lips rejoice when I sing to You, as well as my soul which You have redeemed." (Psalms 71:23)

If you are not happy, start by pretending to be happy. Speak in positive, joyful ways or sing a cheerful tune. Even though your heart is aching with sadness now, keep acting happy; HaShem will redeem you and give you real joy.

"Behold, I am sending My messenger, and he shall clear the way before Me, and HaShem whom you seek shall suddenly come to his chamber..." (Malachi 3:1)

HaShem only resides in a person who has joy. First, clear the way for joy, and then HaShem will follow.

"In all sadness, there is some gain." (Proverbs 14:23)

Even if you are sad and cannot seem to lift yourself from this state, be strong. Know that this too is good and soon your sadness will turn to joy. Just as the past sins of a penitent become like merits for him, so too the sadness of the past will add to the joy you will attain in the near future.

CHAPTER 2:
PEACE

"And you shall not hurt the feelings of one another, but you shall fear your HaShem, for I, HaShem, am your HaShem."
(Leviticus 25:17)

If you hurt another Jew, it is obvious that you lack fear of HaShem. Would you insult a prince in front of the king, unless you didn't fear his punishment? We must have this same respect for our fellow Jew. We must understand that he is a "prince" of HaShem.

"Hatred causes strife, but love draws a cover over all transgressions." (Proverbs 10:12)
If you love your fellow Jew and do kindness to others, then HaShem can't bear to look at your sins, but instead looks only at your merits.

"One who conceals the wrong done to him by a friend will be loved by his friend, and one who repeats this wrong continuously will cause a break in their relationship." (Proverbs 17:9)
Many times, we love our friends so much that we want to help them perfect every quality they possess. A friend must know how tactfully to help his friend grow spiritually. We feel so close to the ones we love, that we think we can

just blurt out whatever we feel. This is far from the truth. For those we are close to, we must use even more restraint.

"When a man's ways please HaShem, He even makes his enemies at peace with him." (Proverbs 16:7)
When others turn away from you, it is a sign that you must refocus your ways and improve your service of HaShem. When you return to HaShem, then others will return in peace to you.

"If your enemy is hungry give him bread to eat and if he is thirsty give him water to drink." (Proverbs 25:21)
It's easy to make peace with those already close to you, but to make peace with your enemy is a sign of true love of HaShem.

"Seek peace and pursue it!" (Psalms 34:15)
People always wait for peace instead of going after it. If you want peace, you must make it happen. Don't wait for it to come to you.

"Therefore, you must love truth and peace." (Zechariah 8:19)
Only those who have a great love for truth also have a desire to pursue peace.

"Better a close neighbor than a brother far away." (Proverbs 27:10)
Whom do we consider a friend? Our natural tendency is to label "friends" as people who give us what we want. It's easier to take from our close family than from friends. Friendships are about giving, not receiving.

"Let your foot be seldom in your neighbor's house lest he be sated with you and hate you." (Proverbs 25:17)

If you want to keep a long-lasting friend, give him reasons to come to your home rather than you visit your friend's home.

"And Amnon hated her with a very great hatred, for the hatred with which he hated her was greater than the love with which he had loved her." (2 Samuel 13:15)

The more we love someone, the stronger our hatred for them can become when the situation changes. This is because we hate them for stealing our love and because we opened our hearts to them, only to have our hearts broken. I wonder if visceral hatred of a family member or friend is actually very deep love in disguise.

"He makes peace in his heavenly heights." (Job 25:2)

Just as HaShem makes peace in His palace, we must make peace within our own palaces. That is, we must make peace between our character traits and emotions. We must strive for balance and a sense of peace.

"They hate me because I pursue good." (Psalms 38:21)

If you have recently started to pursue a life of Torah, watch how others react to your choice. If they seem to hate you because of your decision, it reveals something about their own path. Their path is not a real one. If it were, they would be confident in their own ways and only show love to others.

"I am for peace, but when I speak, they are for war." (Psalms 120:7)

We can learn from the example of King David. No matter how much Saul pursued him, trying to hurt and kill him, he never gave up making peace.

"Truth and a judgment of peace shall you judge in your gates." (Zechariah 8:16)

When we look at others, we should always judge them favorably and assume that they have good intentions. This will bring us peace of mind. Always finding the faults of others only causes us anger and hatred in our hearts.

"He makes peace in your borders and sates you with the fatness of wheat." (Psalms 147:14)
Those who have peace are blessed with wealth.

"It is an honor to a man to abstain from a quarrel." (Proverbs 20:3)
Don't think that participating in a quarrel will cause you to be a winner; understand that abstaining is a much worthier (and difficult) achievement.

"In an abundance of words offense shall not cease, and he who spares his lips is wise." (Proverbs 10:19)
When speaking to those with whom you tend to quarrel, do not prolong the conversation.

"And the humble will inherit the land and they will delight in a plenitude of peace." (Psalms 37:11)
A humble person is always at peace with others. Those with pride are always in conflict with others.

CHAPTER 3:
MUSIC

"A song of ascents: Out of the depths have I cried to You, O' HaShem."(Psalms 130:1)

The true depth of a person is revealed through song. You can talk to HaShem from deep within, but when you sing to HaShem with all your heart, it breaks every obstacle blocking the light of HaShem from you.

"How can we sing the song of HaShem on the soil of an alien [god]?" (Psalms 137:4)
Whenever we sing a song, we should hope for the time when we will sing in the comfort of the *Bais Hamikdosh*. Otherwise, how can we sing?

"I will rise at midnight to praise you…" (Psalms 119:62)
When a person praises someone sincerely, his speech does not come out in a normal tone; rather, it comes forth musically.

"Serve HaShem with joy, come before Him with song." (Psalms 100:2)
If you are obligated to do something, it must be done regardless of your attitude, so why not complete the task

joyously? If you come before HaShem in prayer, why not compose it to Him like a beautifully arranged, heartfelt song?

"Then Moses and the children of Israel chose to sing this song to HaShem." (Exodus 14:32)
When you are with others, choose a tune fitting for your friends, and not just one that you enjoy.

"Then Moses sang..." (Exodus 15:1)
A person sings after having been emotionally touched by something.

"Praise Him with sounding cymbals! Praise Him with loud clashing cymbals!" (Psalms 150:5)
All other instruments are mentioned only once, but the Tanach mentions cymbals twice. This is because, when you make music, it is understandable and acceptable to be loud like a cymbal; as long as it doesn't bother someone else.

"Give thanks to HaShem, call upon His name, make His works known amongst the peoples, sing to Him, make music for Him, and speak of all His wonders." (Psalms 105:1-2)
A person can express feelings about something through words, but through music and song, one's sincere appreciation comes forth.

"I am for HaShem. I will sing and praise HaShem of Israel." (Judges 5:3)
People with strong beliefs may feel a great need to express those feelings that are bursting inside of them. This is why many people with strong convictions become musicians and artists.

"A song of the *shabbos* day. It is good to thank HaShem and to sing praise to your Name, O' Exalted One." (Psalms 92:1)

For every situation and mood, there is an appropriate song.

"They will praise His name with dance, with a drum and a harp they will sing to Him." (Psalms 149:3)

To the musician or dancer, music is a prayer said silently in one's mind while its words are expressed from within.

"Then shall the trees of the forest sing out at the presence of HaShem because He comes to judge the earth." (Chronicles I 16:33)

Those who look beneath the surface can hear the trees, and other forms of nature whistling and dancing in the wind, as one would dance to music.

"Let the rivers clap their hands, let the mountains sing for joy together!" (Psalms 98:8)

We are a disjointed people. It's impossible for us to appreciate the music that nature creates because we can't imagine that such a unity exists.

"And as singers who are like dancers are all those who study You." (Psalms 87:7)

People sing with their physical body as a way of expressing their soul - which all the while has been dancing.

"Then Moses and the Children of Israel sang this song to HaShem, and they said, 'I shall sing to HaShem, for He has triumphed; He has thrown the horse and its rider into the sea.'" (Exodus 15:1)

A person sings after being victorious. That is, after awakening a quiet soul.

"Let the wilderness and its cities lift up their voice, the village that Kedar inhabits; let the inhabitants of the rocks sing, let them shout from the peaks of the mountains. Let them give glory to HaShem and tell of His praise in the islands." (Isaiah 42:11-12)

Someone who has been asleep from doing the will of HaShem is similar to a rock that is still. When that person bursts out in song, it brings tremendous glory to HaShem – even more than that of one who was already awake.

"From the wings of the land we have heard song, glory to the righteous." (Isaiah 24:16)

Tzaddikim are like the wings of *Klal Yisrael*. They take the prayers and actions of *Klal Yisrael* and lift them up as a beautifully composed song.

"For HaShem will comfort Zion, He will comfort all her ruined areas, and He will make her wilderness like Eden and her desert like the garden of HaShem; joy and gladness shall be found in her, thanksgiving and the sound of melody." (Isaiah 51:3)

When a person is comforted after a lengthy period of suffering, his gladness is like music to him and to those around him.

CHAPTER 4: MARRIAGE

"A good wife, who so finds; her worth is far above rubies. The heart of her husband trusts in her. Her children rise up and call her blessed." (Proverbs 31:10)

Each man's wife is a good wife for him, chosen specifically for him by HaShem. He must look for this good, but most importantly, he must recognize the goodness in her that she already possesses. When he sees this good, he will trust her and realize that her worth is invaluable to him.

"He, who finds a wife, finds good." (Proverbs 18:22)
A single person can have a very good life, but you can't truly taste goodness unless you share it with someone you love more than yourself.

"Charm is deceptive, and beauty is vain; but a woman who fears HaShem, she shall be praised." (Proverbs 31:30)
When a person fears HaShem, the *Shechinah* rests on that person. Being attached to the *Shechinah* is very holy and brings a person grace. This grace is not only a physical state but also a spiritual smoothness and gracefulness that can't be described in words.

"A good wife is a crown to her husband, but one who acts shamefully is like rot in his bones." (Proverbs 12:4)

A woman is a crown to her husband when he elevates her with the proper *kavod*, which she deserves. When he treats her as his servant, she will act shamefully to bring him disrespect. She will bring him more misery and unhappiness than anything else could.

"It is better to live in a corner of the roof than share a large house with a quarrelsome wife." (Proverbs 21:9)

The home is the woman's domain. Only a small corner belongs to the husband. Instead of making a quarrel, always return to your corner and then make peace.

"A quarrelsome wife is like a constant drip." (Proverbs 27:15)

It's very difficult for people who are used to quarreling to stop themselves. Even if they would like to change this *middah*, it can take a lifetime. If you want to seal a leak, you must plug the leak with something. With your spouse, you must plug that leak with unconditional love. Eventually, it will no longer drip.

"I gave my daughter to this man." (Deuteronomy 22:16)

One of the most difficult things for a parent is to "give" a daughter to a man. The parents have spent many years protecting their daughter, and now they must relinquish this responsibility to her husband. Worry never leaves the heart of a parent. He has to keep on reminding himself to let go.

"I am for my beloved and my beloved is for me." (Song of Songs 6:3)

Only when a person nullifies his or her own ego in order to give to another does the other person do the same.

You can't expect a spouse to be devoted to you when you fail to devote yourself to your spouse.

"Enjoy life with the wife whom you love all the day of the life of your vanity..." (Ecclesiastes 9:9)

It is important for a couple to do joyous things together. Unfortunately, many marriages fail simply from a lack of effort. Couples must want to enjoy life with one another. Make a conscious effort to bring happiness into your home and out of your home. Make a "date-night", on a fixed schedule, when you and your spouse go out, and enjoy each other's company.

"Many waters cannot quench love; neither can the floods drown it." (Song of Songs 8:7)

Love should be something unbreakable. An argument should just be that; an argument. It should not affect one's love and affection for the other. If it does, then a person must work on loving more.

"And I (HaShem) will betroth you (Israel) to Me forever." (Song of Songs 2:21)

We can learn from HaShem how to love our spouse. HaShem's love for us is unconditional and never ceases, not even for a moment.

"Jacob loved Rachel." (Genesis 29:18)

The truest love is one that grows on a person, not one that is spontaneous.

"A helpmate opposite..." (Genesis 2:18)

Sometimes a man and wife will have opposite opinions on an issue. When one is opposite the other, they are directly across from each other. This is actually a very strong position. They will now be able to cover twice as much ground as a couple that agrees.

This can be compared to two study partners in a Jewish house of study. If they both agree on how to understand the text, they delve only into that approach. If one study partner understands the text differently than the other, they will now be able to learn from two approaches.

"When a man acquires a wife..." (Deuteronomy 24:1)
A man must feel that his wife is completely devoted to him. Otherwise, he feels alone. Not that she should belittle herself for him, but to the best of her ability, she should help him feel confident of her love.

"And he shall cleave unto his wife." (Genesis 2:24)
Many women who feel insecure shut out their husbands emotionally. Thus, each pushes the other away, like two magnets repelling each other. If they would just turn around, they would cleave strongly.

"Love your neighbor as yourself." (Leviticus 19:18)
A person must work on nullifying his own ego for another. If you are not kind to your neighbor, then you won't know how to be kind to your spouse.

"And she took her veil and covered herself." (Genesis 24:64)
A woman has to cover herself, meaning she should be content with her life as a wife and mother. When she starts complaining, there will be no end to it. Instead, she should go about her life happily. When she is modest and accepting of her lot, then her greatness will be revealed to her husband. If she is not, he will not see her in the proper light.

"When a man takes a new wife, he shall be deferred from military duty, he shall not be charged with any business, he shall be free for his house one year, and shall cheer his wife whom he has taken." (Deuteronomy 24:5)

When a woman needs to be cheered up, her husband should stop everything and tend to her. Once she is content, he can return to his affairs. If not, the unhappiness in his home will build up to such a point that he will have to abandon all outside affairs permanently. With her happiness comes blessing, but her sadness is like a curse that must be immediately undone.

CHAPTER 5:
ANGER

"The lion is the mightiest of animals and turns away before no one."
(Proverbs 30:30)

The lion is the king of all the other animals and with this power, there is great responsibility. It uses its *middah*, character trait, of ferociousness to lead the other animals in the proper way. So too with HaShem - what seems like anger to us is a proper *middah* to keep us in order.

"The forcing of wrath brings forth strife." (Proverbs 30:33)
It is remarkable how often we say and do things, knowing how much it will hurt another person. That is even if it is something frivolous.

"A man of great wrath shall suffer punishment." (Proverbs 19:19)
If you are angry over frivolous things, HaShem will instead give you things which you could really be angry about.

"It is the wisdom of a man that restrains his anger." (Proverbs 19:11)
If a person would think more first, it would be impossible to reach the point of anger. Why? Because anger

doesn't help a person; it just makes it harder to come up with a solution.

"For the fool is killed by anger." (Job 5:2)
Anger destroys the holy life force inside a person. Without the holy life force, a person is like a dead man.

"Do not become friendly with one who has a temper, and do not come together with a wrathful person." (Proverbs 22:24)
Angry people remove the *Shechinah* from themselves and from those around them. Therefore, it is wise to stay away from such a person, especially during his fits.

"And the man of anger is abundant in sin." (Proverbs 29:22)
If someone is known to be an angry person, there is a good chance that he also indulges often in forbidden physical pleasures.

"He, who waxes in anger, bears his punishment." (Proverbs 19:19)
A person who has significant amounts of anger also has significant amounts of strength to undergo more punishment for his wrongdoings. When a calm person sins, HaShem helps bear the burden of the punishment.

"A man's intellect is the withholding of his anger." (Proverbs 19:11)
Angry people cannot receive and process information well in the heat of the moment. Holding back anger gives a person tremendous understanding in that moment when he or she doesn't get angry.

"Do not hate your brother in your heart." (Leviticus 19:17)

People are fooled to believe that anger kept within is not true anger. It is quite the contrary; it is the most virulent form of anger.

"Let there not be in you a strange god." (Psalms 81:10)

Anger is a form of idolatry. If you are angry with any person, thing, or life event - these are all included in HaShem, so, therefore, your anger is directed at Him.

"He who covers over the faults of others seeks to maintain love, but he who keeps repeating an action breaks up a friendship." (Proverbs 17:9)

Everyone has faults. To constantly reprove a person because you are angry at an imperfection, truly shows your own imperfection with anger.

"One who is slow to anger is greater than a strong man." (Proverbs 16:32)

The real strength of a person is the ability to control his emotions.

"A gentle response turns away anger; a negative response increases anger." (Proverbs 15:1)

We should act gently in resolving all matters. An angry response shows the elevated level of pride with which we regard ourselves.

"Better is he who withholds his wrath than the hero, and he who rules his spirit than the conqueror of a city; and withholding of wrath is one of the thirteen attributes stated in relation to the Blessed Creator." (Proverbs 16:32)

The forces of impurity that stem from losing one's temper are so strong, that it takes a warrior to silence them. He is like a hero as he saves damage to his soul and those who would be affected by him.

"In anger, you remembered mercy." (Habakkuk 3:2)

HaShem's anger is not similar to that of flesh and blood. HaShem's anger is filled with *chesed* because of His mercy.

"The wicked man, when his anger grows, [says that] He [HaShem] will not inquire [after my deeds]." (Psalms 10:4)

An angry person has pride and therefore feels he is not responsible for his actions.

CHAPTER 6:
CHARITY

"And from your flesh and blood, you shall not look away."(Isaiah 58:7)

It is important to help everyone, but sometimes we overlook those close to us. At times, we might hurt them in the process of giving to someone else. It is certainly good to give to others, but family should always come first.

"But you shall surely open your hand to him and shall surely lend him enough for his need." (Deuteronomy 15:8)
Don't just give people what they ask for on the surface. Make sure to give a person what he or she truly needs. There are times when a person may come to you for money or for help in finding a soul mate, but he needs something else. We must take notice of others and see if there is another unspoken request beneath the surface.

"A man's wealth will redeem his soul." (Proverbs 13:8)
When you give charity to any organization, you become part of everything it accomplishes. There may have once been a young boy whose school you supported, and that boy grew up and became a great Torah scholar. You own a piece of the Heavenly reward that he gets from every lesson

he teaches. There are tremendous merits that accumulate over the years from charity.

"In the path of charity there is life; in the way it leads, there is no death." (Proverbs 12:28)

When a person loses money, it can be compared to death, as in many ways, a poor man is considered dead. One cannot lose by giving charity to worthy causes. Giving charity is a safeguard against your poverty.

"He who closes his ears to the cry of the poor will himself cry out and not be heard." (Proverbs 21:13)

There are very few guarantees as to whether an individual prayer will be answered. Certainly, the giving of *tzedakah*, is a powerful expression of love, not only to the recipient but also to HaShem. If you saw your own son give to another with so much love and sweetness, wouldn't you reward him?

"And your charity shall go before you." (Isaiah 48:8)

Whenever people are nervous about some event, they send a scout to check out the situation first. Charity can be our "scout"; we should always give it before we approach HaShem. It will then open the door for everything else that takes place thereafter.

"Will you not break your bread to the hungry?" (Isaiah 58:7)

Other *mitzvos* don't really require the breaking of oneself as does the giving of charity. When you give charity, you are taking your very sustenance and sharing it with others. For some, it's comparable to giving over their very life.

"Happy is he who considers the poor; on a day of evil, HaShem will deliver him." (Psalms 41:2)

The charity that a person gives will always stand by him during times of judgment.

"If there be among you a poor man of one of your brothers in one of your gates in your land that HaShem, your HaShem gives to you, do not close your hand to your poor brother." (Deuteronomy 15:7)

If the poor man is one of your brothers, then obviously he is in your gates. Your gates are obviously in your land. Why, then, are all these phrases used? HaShem is very subtly reminding us that everything we have comes from Him and therefore, we should not be stingy with the poor.

"One man gives freely yet grows all the richer; another withholds what he should give and only suffers want." (Proverbs 11:24)

It is natural for people to assume that possessing money will solve their yearnings. This is not the case. The only person who money brings happiness, is the person who gives it away.

"He who is gracious to the poor lends to HaShem, and He will pay him his reward." (Proverbs 19:17)

Everything we own truly belongs to HaShem. We have been appointed HaShem's accountants to distribute His money to the proper sources. By doing HaShem's will and using one's possessions to help others, HaShem rewards us by entrusting us with even more of His resources.

"Treasures of wickedness profit nothing but righteousness delivers from death." (Proverbs 10:2)

When a person has many possessions and hoards them, these "treasures" are fruitless. If a person gives constantly of himself, his life becomes very meaningful. A person is not really living unless he or she performs acts of righteousness on a regular basis.

"He loves righteousness and justice; the earth is full of the loving-kindness of HaShem." (Psalms 33:3)

When a person doesn't give of himself to others, then the world is closed to him. If one gives to others, then the world opens for him. The more you give, the more the world's doors unlock!

"The generous man will be enriched, and he who satiates will himself be satiated." (Proverbs 11:25)

When a person is poor, it is HaShem testing him to see if He can trust him with His treasures. As soon as He sees he can be trusted with a little, HaShem gives him a little more. The more trustworthy, the more He continues to give him. How do you gain HaShem's trust? By giving!

Hashem says, "On account of the oppression of the poor, on account of the sighing of the needy, now I will arise. I will grant deliverance." (Psalms 12:5)

It is easy for those with sufficient means to offer praise to HaShem. When those who are lacking look to HaShem, their sighs and prayers go through all the gates. It is through their simple cry that deliverance descends to the world.

"Bring offerings of charity and trust in HaShem." (Psalms 4:6)

What is the purpose of a *korban*, an offering to HaShem? It is to take something dear to us, a piece of our livelihood, and give it back to HaShem. This is the ultimate expression of faith.

"You shall surely give Him, and your heart shall not be grieved when you give to Him; because for this thing HaShem, your HaShem, shall bless you in all your works, and in all that to which you put your hand." (Deuteronomy 15:10)

Normally when a person spends money, he feels grief in his heart. This is because he is so attached to his money that he feels a tremendous loss. This is not the case when a person gives charity. Even if we don't always see the rewards of charity in the physical world, HaShem imbues the giver's *neshama*, with extra joy.

"Well will it be with the man who is kind and lends his money; he will guide his affairs with justice." (Psalms 112:5)

There are people who give with a happy countenance; but inside, they are not giving with all their heart. A person who gives with the sweetness of his heart, all his affairs will be completed with blessing.

CHAPTER 7:
CHILDREN

"Children's children are the crown of old men." (Proverbs 17: 6)

A crown is worn to show stature and nobility. Having grandchildren who go in the ways of HaShem is the greatest accomplishment.

"A wise son is a joy to his father." (Proverbs 10:1)
A parent's main joy is watching his child's intelligence grow, becoming the person he is meant to be.

"Your children are like olive plants around your table." (Psalms 128:3)
Olives can be made into either extra - refined oil or lesser quality oil. It all depends on the processing. The same goes for children; it all depends on how they have been educated.

"Condition the youth according to his way; then even when he grows old it will not desert him." (Proverbs 22:6)
If children are used to being around holy parents who are devoted to HaShem, then that will feel normal for them.

"You shall be holy to Me, for I, HaShem, am holy, and I have set you apart from all other peoples, that you should be Mine." (Leviticus 20:26)

Just like HaShem set apart His children, raising them above all other nations, so too we must make our children feel that they are most important to us.

"Be fruitful and multiply; fill up the earth and rule over it." (Genesis 1:28)

Children extend our value and worth. We see that the more children one has, the more powerful his family becomes. One person has only so many connections and can affect only so many people, but many together are far stronger. Raising children takes one's strength but it also opens up doors that are otherwise closed.

"The rod of correction creates wisdom, but a child left to his self, brings disgrace to his mother." (Proverbs 10:1)

Without the fear of correction, a person can't even begin to serve HaShem. He might try but does not have enough wisdom to overcome his negative character traits.

"He, who spares the rod, hates his son." (Proverbs 13:24)

Many times, when we should really be embracing our children, we punish them. When we should rebuke them, we embrace them. A parent should find an appropriate balance of discipline, depending on the needs of the child. It is certainly wrong to be completely merciful.

"As arrows in the hand of a mighty man, so are the children of one's youth." (Psalms 127:4)

Children help their parents to see themselves in a realistic light. By raising a family early in life, a person strengthens his or her character far more than the older adult already set in his ways. We learn so much from our children.

"Have I not calmed and quieted my soul; like a weaned child my soul is with me." (Psalms 131:2)

Even at times when we take the holiness of our souls for granted, HaShem is still watching over us as a mother does her nursing infant. As we mature and calm the negative spirits within us, our soul is shown its own strength - similar to a child being weaned from its mother.

"Israel is My child, My firstborn." (*Exodus* 4:22)

Siblings usually follow the first-born's example. Therefore, it's very important to raise one's firstborn to be an excellent role model.

"May He bless the lads and let them carry my name along with the names of my fathers." (Genesis 48:16)

It's a big responsibility to carry on the name of your family. You need strength and blessing to live up to the merit of previous generations.

"Train a lad in the way he ought to go; he will not swerve from it even in old age." (Proverbs 22:6)

Many parents try to fulfill their dreams through their children instead of helping their children forge a new, unique identity.

"Come, children, listen to me; I will teach you the fear of HaShem." (Psalms 34:12)

Learning to fear HaShem takes much discipline and education from the wise. If only we would instill this in our children at an early age, it would remain with them as they mature. A child learns fear of HaShem by watching his parents and teachers.

"If I raised my hands against the fatherless… may my arm drop off my shoulder." (Job 31:21, 22)

We must be very gentle with those who have lost a parent. Their souls are very fragile, and we must support them by making them a part of our own families.

"Perhaps my children have sinned and blasphemed HaShem in their thoughts." (Job 1:5)
A parent has difficulty accepting the imperfections of his children; maybe this is because it is also his own imperfection.

"And make them known to your children and your children's children." (Deuteronomy 4:9)
We have to understand the power of raising children in the ways of HaShem. When we teach them the right way, then they teach their peers and their children. Then, they, in turn, teach it to their children and peers and spread the teachings even further. Therefore, there is no end to the blessing that descends into the world when you bring up children in the ways of HaShem.

"She looks well to the ways of her household." (Proverbs 31:27)
It's important for a mother to not only care for the household but to look, and truly see, that the path her children take will lead them to righteousness.

CHAPTER 8:
FAITH AND TRUST

"Though He slays me, yet I will trust in Him." (Job 13:15)

Come what may, one must always place complete trust in HaShem. Your best friend, wife or your children could turn against you, Heaven forbid, but do not worry. This is a signal from HaShem that He wants you to search your heart. You only exist because of HaShem's constant kindness. Therefore, it is only fitting to trust HaShem completely.

"Blessed is the man who trusts in HaShem and whose hope HaShem is." (Jeremiah 17:7)
It is not enough to believe that every life event comes from HaShem. One must also believe that salvation is coming soon. When you trust in someone, it means that you are willing to give a part of your soul over to him or her. That is why when someone breaks your trust you are hurt so much. It is because they have snatched part of your soul. If you entrust your soul to HaShem, He will return it full of blessing.

"Trust in HaShem with all your heart and lean not to your own understanding." (Proverbs 3:5)
When unusual events happen in life, it is natural for people to come up with their own explanations. This gives

people a feeling of control over the situation. When you truly trust in HaShem, you do not have to turn toward your own understanding. The acceptance with full trust that everything comes from HaShem means you do not need to use your own reasoning.

"Trust in HaShem and do good so you shall dwell in the land and be nourished by [your] faith." (Psalms 37:3)

You cannot live a productive life without faith. Faith has a calming effect on a person and this nourishes the entire body. It gives a person the necessary tools to advance both physically and spiritually.

"And they that know My name will put their trust in Me." (Psalms 9:11)

People will not put their trust in a person they do not know. But how does one get to know HaShem? Well, if you wanted to get close to an important person, what would you do? You would find out who knows him and draw close to that person, hoping he will draw you close to the person you are truly seeking to know. Those who already "know" HaShem are the *tzaddikim* - the righteous leaders of our generation.

King David said, "The way of trust, I have chosen; Your mandates I have set before me." (Psalms 119:30)

In every situation, you have many options available. Trusting in HaShem isn't the easiest option, but it is the greatest guarantee of success.

Concerning Moses our teacher, it is written, "In my entire house he is the faithful." (Numbers 12:7)

Whom would you want as a best friend? A person who believes in you! Moses was the most faithful of all of HaShem's creations. Therefore, it was Moses whom HaShem drew closest to Him, by talking to him through the burning bush.

"For HaShem will help me, therefore I am not confounded." (Isaiah 50:7)

A person who doesn't believe in HaShem will always be confused. He will not know whether to go towards the right or the left. When you trust in HaShem, even if you go left when you should have gone right, you will end up where you need to be.

"He who trusts in HaShem, loving-kindness surrounds him." (Psalms 32:10)

If you put trust in something, and your trust is fulfilled, then you will celebrate all the kindness that has been done for you. If you go through life without trust in HaShem, then the good things He does for you, will go unnoticed. Therefore, you will never feel His loving kindness that is truly there at all times.

"Trust in HaShem and do good; dwell in the land and cultivate faith." (Psalms 37:3)

You should constantly try to improve your faith in HaShem. Just as land must be tilled and cultivated, so must we continuously work on our faith in HaShem. We can do this by trusting in HaShem and doing *mitzvos*.

"And the people believed." (Exodus 4:31)

It seems to be such a remarkable thing that the people believed. Of course, they should have believed. HaShem gives one sign after another to us and yet we forget? We need to see more signs to know that he is there with us. Why can't we remember what we have already seen? HaShem, in His complete understanding of human nature, takes into account this flaw and frequently sends us signs to strengthen us.

"Have I not commanded you? Be strong and of good courage; be not afraid, neither be dismayed: for HaShem, your HaShem, is with you wherever you go." (Joshua 1:9)

To follow HaShem's commandments, one must be strong and courageous. Do not be scared of the Satan or of the vicissitudes you will experience. HaShem says, "I will always be there beside you even when you fall. So, place your trust in Me; I will not fail you, nor forsake you." (Deuteronomy 31:6)

"Blessed is the man who trusts and relies upon HaShem." (Jeremiah 17:1)

If a mortal king would see one of his subjects devoting himself exclusively to serving the king, it seems natural that the king would provide the resources necessary for this service. The same is true with HaShem; if we rely on Him totally, He will give us everything we need in life.

"Cast unto HaShem your burden, and He will sustain you." (Psalms 55:23)

HaShem doesn't want us to worry about our difficulties in life. He would rather we give them over to Him trustingly. Don't keep your problems to yourself. Once you have made a reasonable effort, give your burden to HaShem. He knows what to do with it better than you do!

"And as for me, in Your loving kindness, I have trusted." (Psalms 13:6)

By trusting in HaShem's loving kindness, we arouse HaShem's mercy. With mercy, HaShem sustains all creatures and gives them sustenance. Patiently, a bird flies through the sky looking for food, confident that HaShem will provide its needs. We too must trust in the lovingkindness of HaShem.

"Cursed is the man who puts his faith in man." (Jeremiah 17:5)

Since HaShem is infinite and beyond the grasp of our understanding, it is easy to feel that He is inaccessible to us. If we put our faith in man for our answers, we are bound to lose. Man is only a creation of HaShem and has no independent power. Therefore, we must place our trust in HaShem alone. We may use the help of man to assist us, but certainly, our faith should be in the Almighty.

"HaShem of Hosts, fortunate is the man who trusts in You." (Psalms 84:13)

Whenever the name "HaShem of Hosts" is used, it is alluding to the completion of judgment from HaShem. Especially fortunate is the person who currently has faith in HaShem. The name "HaShem of Hosts" will then ease the tribulation. (Sha'are Orah, The Fifth Gate)

"Trust and rely upon Him at all times." (Psalms 62:9)

It's common for people to trust in HaShem, only when convenient for them. One should trust in HaShem always, especially when things are most difficult. When trust in HaShem seems to come far too easy for a person, maybe it is then he should evaluate if his trust is real.

CHAPTER 9:
FEAR OF HASHEM

"The beginning of wisdom is the fear of HaShem." (Proverbs 1:7)

This simple verse contains the entire key to serving HaShem. Let us begin by contemplating what it means to make a beginning. When you start from scratch, how you begin sets the foundation for everything that comes afterward. Solomon, the wisest of all men, teaches us that, if you want wisdom, forget everything you already know. If you don't fear HaShem, you haven't tasted true wisdom. All you have learned until now is simply meaningless. It isn't true knowledge at all. The entire goal of knowledge must be to increase one's fear of Heaven.

"The end of the matter, all having been heard, is to fear HaShem, and keep His commandments, for this is the whole of man." (Ecclesiastes 12:13)
A vessel without any holes can hold liquid without leaking. Fear of Heaven turns a person into a whole vessel. Without fear of Heaven, blessings can wash over you but, like a vessel with even one hole, everything will simply spill out.

"Better a little with the fear of the HaShem, then great treasure and confusion therewith." (Proverbs 15:16)

A person can accomplish remarkable things in service to HaShem; but if one lacks the fear of HaShem that should manifest in the heart, he will constantly fall into confusion. It is fear of HaShem that enables one to contemplate his lowliness compared to HaShem's infinite greatness. The confusion stems from too much pride in oneself. A person only has pride when he lacks fear and awe of the Omnipresent One.

"I have set HaShem before me always; because He is at my right hand I shall not falter." (Psalms 16:8)
If you place yourself in the right surroundings, it will be easy to grow and not be affected by negative influences. Make a protective fence around yourself, so as not to falter. We are standing constantly before the Omnipresent One and must constantly remember this by "setting Him before our eyes". To do this, we must live among those who are close to HaShem.

"The fear of HaShem is His treasure." (Isaiah 33:6)
It's not love of HaShem, or trust in Him, but rather fear that is compared to a treasure. To fear HaShem is to know Him. When a wealthy person talks about his riches, he doesn't mention his coins of silver and copper. Rather, he talks about his gold. Fear of HaShem is like gold in a treasure box. Though other coins might be important and there might be more of them, gold attracts the attention. HaShem is telling us to fear Him since this is the main treasure.

"The fear of HaShem is pure; it endures forever." (Psalms 19:10)
Today, everything seems to contain some mixture of chemicals to preserve its shelf life. When it comes to fear of HaShem, you don't need to add artificial preservatives. Let your fear of HaShem be simple and pure. This alone will make a profound impression on your heart, and it will stand by you forever.

"And HaShem has wrought so that men should fear Him." (Ecclesiastes 3:14)

Every action that takes place in the world is in order that fear of HaShem should be known. Unfortunately, we blind ourselves from this simple realization. If only we could understand that, each movement comes from Heaven. Somewhere in the subconscious mind is true fear of HaShem. Our goal in life is to bring this into the conscious mind.

"Lift up your eyes on high and see Who has created these." (Isaiah 40:26)

When Ben Azai (Talmud Chagigah 14b) saw the awesome greatness of the angel Metatron, he thought it had power in its own right. This was wrong since its entire power is derived only from HaShem. An angel cannot accomplish even the simplest deeds if HaShem did not decree it so.

Conversely, when Rabbi Akiva entered the *Pardes*, he clung to the knowledge that HaShem is infinite. Because of this, he entered and left in peace. When we leave this world and come before HaShem for our final judgment, we will see who was truly behind every test and situation that we encountered in life. It will then be clear to us Who created everything. Let us not wait for the final judgment day to realize "Who has created these". Instead, "let us lift up our eyes on high" with a pure fear of HaShem.

"Come, children, listen to me; I will teach you fear of HaShem." (Psalms 34:12)

The verse could have simply been written, "Come, children; I will teach you fear of HaShem." Instead, the words 'listen to me' are added, to stress the importance of teaching this principle to children while they are young. It is common for parents to assume that their children will understand certain principles naturally. This is not so with fear of Heaven. We must teach this right away to our children and especially when they are young.

"HaShem knows the thoughts of man." (Psalms 94:11)

Every thought a person has comes directly from HaShem. A negative thought appears in order to be cast aside and pushed away. Positive thoughts come for the person to embrace. A person's thoughts are very much affected by what he sees, hears, and touches in life. One must build an atmosphere that will have a positive effect on this process. The mind is constantly flowing. If we bind ourselves to fear of HaShem, our very being will be ignited like fire to do HaShem's will.

"Hear, O' Israel, HaShem is our G-d, HaShem is One." (Deuteronomy 6:4)

Klal Yisrael, My holy nation: for some reason you haven't been listening to what is going on around you. All the signs and wonders I have done should certainly be enough to recognize my Oneness and power. Why do you choose to close your ears?

"To fear this honored, awesome Name, YKVK Elokim." (Deuteronomy 28:59)

Everything in the world derives sustenance from HaShem through his name YKVK. (Sha'are Orah, The Fifth Gate)

It is beyond us to understand how we can bless HaShem's Name and not be immediately struck with awe of His greatness. When the holy Rabbi of Tosh prayed, you could even see his little toes quiver from reverence. A person cannot fear the holy Name of HaShem if he recites it rushed, without concentration. You know why we don't quiver like this holy Rebbe? It is because we are not really saying HaShem's Name. If we did, it would be impossible for any limb of our body not to shake.

"Happy is the man who fears always: but he who hardens his heart shall fall into mischief." (Proverbs 28:14)

There is no logical reason in the world why a person shouldn't fear Heaven every second. The only explanation is that we hardened our hearts. Each of us must reflect and figure out why we are pushing HaShem away. Having fear of Heaven should be always; it should not come and go when convenient.

"Fear not; for HaShem has come to test you, so that his fear is upon your faces, that you not sin." (Exodus 20:17)

HaShem is telling us, "You are going to be tested - and that is part of living. Do not fear the tests that you receive in life; rather be bold and strong. I believe in you. That is why I have placed these tests before you. It is in order that you should overcome them and grow as a person. You are to fear Me and not your evil inclination." When fear of Heaven is in your heart, it will be impossible to falter.

"Princes pursued me for naught and my heart feared at Your word." (Psalms 119:161)

When insulted and attacked by peers, that is the time to remember the fear of HaShem. Not one thing can take place on earth that wasn't decreed in Heaven. There may be no logical reason that this person is attacking; therefore, we must remember that HaShem is the prime cause of everything.

"The fear of HaShem increases days." (Proverbs 10:27)

Why does it say, "increases days" instead of "increase years"? It's because someone who fears HaShem doesn't live in the future. He overcomes obstacles one day at a time. Fear of HaShem may not increase the quantity of your days, but it will increase their quality.

"And their fear of Me is a commandment of men learned by rote." (Isaiah 29:13, 14)

Many Jews think that they have, fear of HaShem. However, their inner motives for service are flawed. They are serving HaShem simply to look good in their Torah observant communities. One who has a real fear of HaShem spends every second of his life, thinking about the best way to serve his Creator.

"The base man says in his heart, there is no HaShem." (Psalms 14:1)

So many of us do the will of HaShem, but when it really comes down to it, do we honestly recognize HaShem as we should? How much of our regular religious routine is genuine? We must purify our hearts and inspect every inch of belief.

CHAPTER 10:
HEALING

"For the life of the flesh is in the blood." (Leviticus 17:11)

The soul connects itself to the blood of a person. The flesh draws its life from the blood. If the soul is hurt by a person's sins, then the blood absorbs impurities and the body is afflicted by the lack of pure flowing blood. Therefore, we must seek a spiritual healer, a *tzaddik*, who can prescribe a remedy for our souls.

"Restore the soul." (Psalms 19:8)
A person who sins becomes physically ill because of the weakened connection between body and soul. Why would the soul want to be close to someone who isn't acting in holiness? Sincere repentance restores the soul, and actually makes the connection stronger than it was before the sin.

"I am HaShem, your Healer." (Exodus 1:26)
You hear many people complaining that they can't find a good doctor. HaShem is the only doctor; medical professionals are simply His agents.

"A happy heart is good for healing." (Proverbs 17:22)
Why is joy such an important part of the healing process? It is because the joy of the soul is what strengthens

the bond between body and soul. A person is sick because the connection between body and soul is weakened.

"Through my flesh, I see HaShem." (Job 19:26)
Sometimes only through the ordeal of sickness can one truly connect to HaShem. If so, why should we complain?

"Their heart will understand, and they will repent and be healed." (Isaiah 6:10)
First, we must understand the gravity of our sins and find a solution to prevent them from happening again. Only then can we repent with a full heart, and healing will naturally follow.

"For the life of the flesh is in the blood." (Leviticus 17:11)
When a person says a blessing with full concentration, the blood comes to purify and sustain the limbs of his body.

"The straight of the heart have joy." (Psalms 97:11)
When a person is healthy, he is easily aroused to be joyous. This is because his heart is balanced. When a person is ill, sadness comes easily because his heart is not straight in its complete devotion to HaShem.

"It is a tree of life for those who hold onto it." (Proverbs 3:18)
One who holds on tightly to the Torah, living by it always, will find it to be a lifeline that gives strength.

"Let us make man in our image, after our likeness." (Genesis 1:26)
HaShem created us in His image, but when we sin, we no longer have this image engraved on us. When we act like royalty, refraining from sin because it is beneath our dignity,

the image of HaShem rests upon us. Should the image of HaShem not be with us, confusion and illness run rampant.

"Their shadow has departed." (Numbers 14:9)

For everything physical, there is a spiritual counterpart. It is like a shadow; when the physical object moves, the shadow follows it. The only time it departs is when the spiritual counterpart is no longer in need. Can you imagine the senselessness of someone who might block his own shadow; making the soul feel unwanted?

"Good news fattens." (Proverbs 15:30)

Good news can heal a person quicker than any medication.

"Above all, guard your heart; for from it is the outpourings of life." (Proverbs 4:23)

When a person's heart is pure, seeking only to do the will of HaShem, an outpouring of life will stem from him and affect many people. When the heart is properly guarded, healing descends to all limbs and sinews.

"For they will add to you length of days, years of life, and peace." (Proverbs 3:1-2)

Unlike a physical remedy, which may give a partial healing, the study of Torah is a complete remedy that leaves no place unturned.

"Fear of HaShem adds length of life." (Proverbs 10:27)

Fear of HaShem lengthens one's life such that a person can accomplish twice as much with the same effort. This is because true strength comes from being connected to HaShem.

"A man's spirit strengthens." (Proverbs 18:14)

People always seek to cure the body when it is actually their soul that strengthens them. Therefore, we should seek to heal our connection to the holy soul more than (or at least as much as) we seek to heal the body.

"I've woken up, and I'm still with You." (Psalms 139:18)

Sometimes we need to experience illness in order to wake up and return to HaShem.

CHAPTER 11:
HUMILITY AND MODESTY

"With the humble is wisdom."(Proverbs 11:2)

We can increase our wisdom by recognizing our lack of knowledge. The more we learn Torah, the more we realize our lack of knowledge. Conversely, secular wisdom generally leads to arrogance. Torah learned properly will only lead us on the path of humility.

"The reward of humility and fear of HaShem are riches, and honor, and life." (Proverbs 22:4)
If we are humble, then honor and riches will run after us in a rewarding way. If we are not lowly in our own eyes, honor, and riches will be destructive. Life is rewarding only when one fears HaShem.

"When they are lowered, you shall say: 'Let them be raised!'" (Job 22:29)
The only way to climb from one spiritual level to the next is to realize our own lowliness at present. When we think of ourselves as being worthy of more than we have, usually we receive nothing. When we realize that we don't even deserve what we have, we are humbled and thereby raised up.

"I dwell... with him who is of a contrite and humble spirit." (Isaiah 57:15)

Only through humility can we reunite our souls with our Creator. Before we entered this world, we were humble, dwelling in the glory of HaShem's majesty. When we entered this world, our natural thoughts turned towards gratifying the pleasures of the body. Through breaking our natural inclinations and pushing away the perspective of self-importance, we can return to our former state; a pure dwelling place for HaShem's glory to reside.

"The abomination of HaShem is all who are proud of heart." (Proverbs 16:5)

There is no bigger a desecration of HaShem's name than walking around with a proud heart. HaShem wants His servants to fulfill His commandments, not to serve themselves.

King David said, "And I will speak of Your testimonies (of Torah) before kings and I will not be ashamed." (Psalms 119:46)

Why is it that we feel ashamed of spreading the Torah of HaShem? It is always so important in our eyes to feel accepted by others. We try to meet their standards to avoid feeling ashamed before them. This all stems from self-pride. A humble man is ashamed when he does not spread HaShem's Torah.

"The lowly of spirit will achieve honor." (Proverbs 29:23)

When we believe that we deserve honor and great things, we end up with nothing. Only when a person is happy and accepts his portion in life, does he then receive honor.

"For though HaShem is high, yet He regards the lowly." (Psalms 138:6)

We must follow HaShem's example. Do not ignore those who aren't as knowledgeable as we are and those who are too poor to help themselves.

"And He gives grace to the humble." (Proverbs 3:34)
One of the greatest qualities is that of grace. When someone has grace, he is at peace within himself. This comes from a person's recognition that everything that happens in the world is HaShem's artistry. We are nothing more than a graceful stroke of His brush. If we accept this, then we are free, and blessing can flow through us.

"He guides the humble in justice and teaches the humble His path." (Psalms 25:9)
When a person is humble, HaShem teaches him secrets of the Torah.

"And I am a worm and not a man, shamed of man and despised of people." (Psalms 22:7)
Why does Dovid Hamelech compare himself to a worm? A worm is a simple creature living in the earth, much of the time hidden from sight. The humble man keeps his deeds as hidden as possible and tries to run away from honor. He does this even if it means burying himself in the dirt at times.

"He who is haughty of eye and proud of heart, with him I cannot abide." (Psalms 101:5)
People who are proud may often get what they seek, but they later find it is not as great as what they expected. This is because HaShem is not with them.

"To the humble He gives favor." (Proverbs 3:34)
HaShem is with the humble person during every step he takes.

"And walk modestly with your HaShem." (Michah 6:8)

When we are modest about ourselves and the actions we take, HaShem walks with us. If we are immodest, thinking we have done remarkable things, then we are not walking with HaShem. Were we not created to simply do His will?

"High and holy do I dwell, and with the oppressed and the humble of spirit." (Isaiah 57:15)

This world has many illusions. We think that the oppressed are the low ones, but in reality, they are the ones lifted up in the heavens.

"For though HaShem is exalted, He still regards the lowly; but the haughty, from afar He admonishes." (Psalms 138:6)

HaShem keeps far from the haughty. He gives them what they want so they will leave Him alone and not try to draw near Him. If they are occupied in satisfying their physical desires, it is as if they don't exist. Just as the souls of the righteous ones live on after death, the souls of the haughty ones are dead, even when their bodies are still alive.

"And the humble shall inherit the land, and they shall delight in an abundance of peace." (Psalms 37:11)

To be able to live in Israel, one needs to have humility. Jews in Israel are constantly tested to see if they are humble enough to continue to dwell in the Holy Land. We shall all be redeemed when we realize how unworthy we are of such a gift as *Eretz Yisrael*. Even as she stands today, desolate of her once incredible beauty, there is still so much there. Only if we are humble can we recognize that her beauty has never diminished; it is just in a concealed state.

"And the man, Moses was very humble." (Leviticus 12:3)

A person who is humble doesn't feel he has to impress others. Moses reached a level where he asked HaShem to blot him out of the Torah and in exchange to forgive the Jewish nation. He didn't feel a need to impress others but rather to make others seem impressive. Many times, we help others out of self-pride. It makes us feel good to lift someone else up while at the same time realizing our superiority over them. We walk around mistaking this for selflessness.

CHAPTER 12:
LOVE

"In all your ways, know Him, and He will straighten your paths."
(Proverbs 3:6)

The only way truly to get to know and understand someone is by strengthening your love for him. The more we love HaShem, the stronger our relationship with Him will be.

"My soul thirsts for HaShem, for the living HaShem." (Psalms 42:3)
Why is the phrase "living HaShem" added? It is enough to say, "My soul thirsts for HaShem." The double phrasing expresses a deep yearning constantly to strengthen this love bond. In this way, must we love and crave HaShem.

"And you shall love HaShem your HaShem, with all your soul and with all your might." (Deuteronomy 6:5)
Why does it say, "all your soul and might"? Should it not say, "With all your soul and body"? Rather, to do the *mitzvos* with one's physical body takes a tremendous amount of strength and love of HaShem.

"I behold Your heavens, the work of Your fingers, the moon and the stars that You have set in place. [I think]

What is [frail] man that You should be mindful of him?"
(Psalms 8:4-5)

If HaShem is so high and great, yet He cares for man,
how much more so should we care for our fellow Jews when
we are no greater than they are.

"Honor your father and mother." (Exodus 20:12)
One cannot properly honor another without love.
Without true love, the honor you give will remain incomplete.

"And you should love your fellow man as yourself."
(Leviticus 19:18)
You can't love another if you do not love yourself. If
you love yourself then you will love your fellow man because
he is included within you.

"Do not envy the man of violence and do not choose
any of his ways." (Proverbs 3:31)
Envy and love are emotions that grow on a person. If
someone or something is not going the right way, turn away
immediately. If others near you are envious, you can also
absorb this negative quality.

"And He said to me, 'You are my servant - Israel; in
you, I will be glorified.'" (Isaiah 49:3)
Some servants do the will of their master because
they have no choice. The Jewish Nation serves HaShem out
of love in order to glorify His Name.

"You that cleave to HaShem, your HaShem, you are
all alive today." (Deuteronomy 4:4)
If your love of HaShem isn't strong, you are like a
stone with no life inside it.

"What can I return to HaShem for all His loving-
kindness to me?" (Psalms 116:12)

If only we recognized all the love and kindness HaShem gives to us! If we did, our only thought would be, "How can I return this good?"

"But as for me, the nearness of HaShem is my good." (Psalms 73:28)

There is no greater feeling than being close to those who love you. Nobody in this world loves you as much as HaShem does.

"I asked one thing from HaShem; that I seek to dwell in HaShem's house all the days of my life." (Psalms 27:4)

The main assurance we seek from our loved ones is that they will never abandon us. This is the promise HaShem has given us. Even if we turn away from Him, we can always return home when we repent of our ways.

"The seed of Abraham, my lover." (Isaiah 41:8)

Someone full of kindness to others must also have a tremendous love of HaShem.

"And Abraham rose early in the morning and saddled his donkey." (Genesis 22:3)

How do you show someone you love him? You are there for him before he even needs to ask you for assistance. In addition, when helping him, you make sure he is satisfied beyond his needs. This was Abraham's way, to give to others before they asked for help.

"For Your sake, we are killed all the day long." (Psalms 44:23)

Elijah was lovesick for HaShem. His love was so strong that HaShem had constantly to revive him, as he would give his every strength to please his Creator. Someone who loves another has truly killed himself, as he is not living for himself. What is the reward of such a person? While still alive, Elijah went by chariot to the Heavens.

"Make yourselves holy and be holy, for I am holy."
(Leviticus 11:44)

It is one thing to do holy actions, but to actually be
holy and live a holy life is much more difficult. HaShem is
saying here that if you love Me, be holy and draw near to Me
because I am holy.

"For Israel was a youth and I loved him." (Hosea
11:1)

If you love someone, then that love should keep your
actions and heart youthful. The youthfulness inside us keeps
us going.

"I have loved you, said HaShem." (Malachi 1:2)

You might think, just because things are difficult, that
HaShem loves you less. On the contrary, He loves you more.

"The lovers of HaShem hate evil." (Psalms 97:10)

If you find yourself embracing evil actions, you
haven't even begun to love HaShem.

CHAPTER 13:
PRAYER

"If you prepare your heart and stretch out your hands towards Him."
(Job 11:13)

Suppose you were to enter an important business meeting for your company. Wouldn't you prepare yourself ahead of time, to make sure you would make a proper presentation? Only then, would you enter the meeting and present it. How much more so should we prepare our hearts and minds before standing in prayer towards the Holy One Blessed be He.

"The King will answer us on the day of our calling." (Psalms 20:10)

This verse can be explained through a *mashal*. A child asked his father for a new bike and the father agreed that he deserves one. The child was overjoyed. The next morning, he jumped out of bed and ran downstairs, expecting to see his shiny new bike sitting there. To his dismay, there was no bike. He later went to his father to ask why his new bike wasn't waiting for him when he awoke.

The father answered that when the child asked for a new bike the father agreed that he deserved one but had in mind to give it to him for his birthday, which wasn't for another five months.

The same thing happens when we pray to HaShem for a need. If we deserve it, HaShem will "answer us on that day..." This doesn't mean we will receive it that second. We will receive it in the right time.

"With his mouth and lips he gave Me honor, but his heart was far from Me." (Isaiah 29:13)

This verse in Isaiah is very pertinent to how we serve HaShem today. How many of us say a blessing after we eat something, and then two seconds later we question ourselves if we said it? Most of us are religious only out of habit. We lack the necessary ingredient of concentration when we carry out our service of HaShem.

"With my voice, I cry to HaShem. With my voice, I make supplication to HaShem. I pour out my complaint before Him. I declare before Him my trouble." (Psalms 142:2-3)

Why does it have to mention, "with my voice"? Obviously, if I am making supplication, I am going to be speaking it. Everyone has an inner voice, a true realness. It is with this that we must call to HaShem.

"If you have prepared your heart, spread out your hands to Him." (Job 11:13)

How many times do we begin our prayers without even realizing before Whom we stand? Spreading the hands is a sign of receiving, but frivolous if you have not prepared your heart first.

"Take with you words and return to HaShem." (Hoshea 14:3)

If you don't feel stronger after praying then you know you haven't prayed properly. When you pray correctly, you are able to "take with you" your prayers that day.

"He will call Me, and I will answer him. I am with him in affliction." (Psalms 91:15)

Even while disciplining a child, the parent is eager to embrace the child if he calls out sincerely.

"Isaac went out to meditate in the field towards evening." (Genesis 4:63)

Why did Isaac go out to a field to pray? When you are standing in a field, you realize how small you really are.

"The children of Israel cried out to HaShem." (Exodus 14:10)

HaShem is very merciful, but when you cry out to him, he is aroused even more in His mercy. That is if we cry to Him like we are His children.

"Call Me, and I will answer you." (Jeremiah 33:3)

Sometimes we just recite the words of prayer. If we would actually call to HaShem with full intention, He would surely answer us.

"Cast your burden upon HaShem, and He will sustain you." (Psalms 55:23)

There is a difference between praying for salvation and actually handing your problems over to HaShem. If you cast your burden upon HaShem, there is nothing more to worry about because HaShem will find the appropriate solution.

"The children of Israel lifted their eyes..." (Exodus 14:10)

When you look straight ahead or down, you can only see so far, but when you look up, you see the furthest because the Heavens are the clearest. This is why we use the analogy of the lifting of the eyes to Heaven. Just as Heaven is infinite, so is HaShem and it is to Him that we look for salvation.

"HaShem is close to all who call Him, to all who call Him in truth." (Psalms 145:18)

When we pray to HaShem, we should think to ourselves, "Did I say even one word truthfully?"

"Let my prayer be set forth as incense before You, the lifting of my hands as the evening sacrifice." (Psalms 141:2)

How does incense give off an odor? It burns a piece of plant-like substance. So too, we must set aflame our hearts, melting the evil attached to us and then lift our hearts to Heaven.

"Isaac entreated HaShem, and HaShem let Himself be entreated." (Genesis 25:21)

If you approach a person with honor and respect, even if they do not agree with you, many times they will leave their own thoughts behind.

"I poured out my soul before HaShem." (1 Samuel 1:15)

Normally when you pour something, you have to make sure it doesn't spill. When you pour out your soul before HaShem, it can be anywhere and at any time and you do not have to worry about pouring it "into" something. Not one word will be wasted or lost.

"I pleaded to HaShem at that time." (Deuteronomy 3:23)

The entire purpose of obstacles in life is for a person to turn to HaShem. Therefore, a person shouldn't wait to turn to HaShem. He should do so immediately in his time of need.

"All my bones will say, 'O HaShem, who is like You.'" (Psalms 35:10)

How does one reach this level of their bones speaking to HaShem? When his prayer is like a sacrifice, meaning that he is willing to give his life to HaShem that very moment, to do His will.

"When you walk through the fire, you will not be burned; and the flame will not kindle upon you." (Michah 43:2)

When you draw close to HaShem in prayer, when the fire burns in your heart so strongly that you feel you could leave this world, worry not because you will not be burnt. HaShem will save you. Continue your quest to seek Him out.

CHAPTER 14:
REPENTANCE

"Return to Me and I will return to you." (Malachi 3:7)

We often tell ourselves that as soon as HaShem sheds His light on us, we will repent. How we fool ourselves into thinking this way. Obviously, it's up to us to make the first step.

"Let your garments always be white." (Ecclesiastes 9:8)

A person shouldn't wait to do *teshuvah* (repentance) and allow the stains of his sins to set into his garment. Rather he should clean himself immediately and return to HaShem. If stains have time to set into place, then they become difficult to remove.

"Return, O' Israel, to HaShem, your HaShem." (Hoshea 14:2)

Know that HaShem should be revered and you should repent out of your fear of Him. Also, know that HaShem is your friend; speak to Him as you would speak to a close friend.

"Give glory to HaShem before it grows dark and before your feet stumble on the mountains of twilight and, while you look for light, He turns it into the shadow of death and makes it gross darkness." (Jeremiah 13:16)

Even though the Garden of Eden is the greatest light and reward, it is still darkness, since there one can no longer give glory to HaShem. Now is the time to show the greatness of HaShem.

"My flesh shudders in awe of You and I have feared Your judgments." (Psalms 119:120)

It is not enough for a person to think about awe of HaShem. A person must etch this fear on his very bones. Concentrate and imagine the fear of HaShem flowing through your bloodstream. Do this until one day you truly feel yourself shuddering at the mere thought of standing before the King of Kings.

"For I know my offenses, and my sin is always before me." (Psalms 51:5)

It is important for a person always to remember his sins so that he avoids situations that may tempt him once again. A person must understand his own weaknesses in order to be on guard by means of his strengths.

"I was ashamed and humiliated because I bore the reproach of my youth." (Yirmeyahu 31:18)

It is very difficult to accept and move on from the mistakes we make when we are young and naive. Nevertheless, we must repent and move forward. We become better people when we choose to put the past behind us.

"Turn me back and I shall be turned." (Jeremiah 31:17)

Sometimes we need HaShem to put us back in our place. It might take a little suffering and rebuke to steer us back to repentance. Would we rather HaShem just ignore us?

"Is this not stored up with me, sealed up in my treasuries?" (Deuteronomy 32:34)

The great light sealed away is repentance. We must constantly search for this light, which is why it is so hard for us to repent wholeheartedly. The keys to repentance are hidden in the Torah.

"Let us search and try our ways and return to HaShem." (Lamentations 3:40)

We can only return to HaShem after fully searching our ways. It is not enough to search and find our wrongs. This is the easy part. The difficult part is trying to get back up. It is only after we get back up and stay there that we have returned to HaShem.

"Because punishment for the evil deed is not meted out quickly, therefore the hearts of men are full within them to do evil." (Ecclesiastes 8:11)

We think it is permitted to sin just a little more, just because we have not yet been rebuked. Is HaShem's delaying of punishment a favor to us or a punishment? He rebukes those closest to him immediately, in this world. If we sin and don't see any sign that HaShem is rebuking us, we have truly become full of evil. We should repent immediately before it's too late.

Rabbi Eliezer said, "Repent the day before you die." (Ethics of our Fathers 2:15)

One of the worst things about sin is the precious time lost that can't be recovered. If we realize the importance of every moment of life, we would repent immediately.

"There is not a righteous man upon earth that does good and sins not." (Ecclesiastes 7:20)

We must strive to be free of sin. However, absolute perfection is impossible because only HaShem can be perfect. If we had the ability to be faultless then we would think of ourselves as G-d like. The expectation of self-perfection can sometimes be a tactic of the evil inclination. Should we not live up to our own expectations, we might sink into depression. Therefore, King Solomon warns us not to take self-perfection too far.

"Wash me thoroughly from my iniquity." (Psalms 51:4)
What would you prefer? To bear the weight of your sins, or let HaShem cleanse your sins so you can feel free? King David is saying here, "I'd rather suffer punishment for my sin than to bear it on my shoulders."

"Wash your heart of evil, Jerusalem." (Jeremiah 4:14)
Torah is compared to water. It is the only thing that will cleanse a person's heart and prevent evil from returning.

"Yet, even now, says HaShem, turn to Me with all your heart, and with fasting, and with weeping, and with lamentation." (Yoel 2:12)
I don't care how far you may have turned from Me. Turn back to Me wholeheartedly and I will accept you with open arms.

"Because I declare my transgression and worry over my sin." (Psalms 38:19)
A person can still worry about his sins even after repenting of them. This is because he is unsure whether the repentance was done wholeheartedly. How can one ever truly know if he has fixed his transgressions? Therefore, it is important to recall them from time to time.

"The sacrifices of HaShem are a broken spirit, a broken and contrite heart, O' HaShem, You will not despise." (Psalms 51:19)
If a person is brokenhearted about his actions, even this can be enough to rectify the sin, with no further actions.

Tovim Meoros

CHAPTER 15:
TORAH

"For a mitzvah is a lamp and Torah, light."(Proverbs 6:22)

The *mitzvos* are like a lamp. In our spiritually murky world, without Torah, there can be no light. The Torah can only shine into those who fulfill what they learn. Study without performance is like holding a bulb in your hands without it screwing it into a lamp. Do you expect it to shine for you?

"If not for the Torah, which must be studied day and night, there would not have been a heaven and earth." (Jeremiah 33:25)
We can see from this that it's not enough to learn only at night or by day. One must set times for learning, both night and day.

"From all my mentors, I have learned." (Psalms 119:99)
It's not enough to just learn from the person whose opinion you value the most. Every person has a special ingredient that nobody else has. Learn from that special part of every person.

"Moses commanded us a law, an inheritance of the congregation of Jacob." (Deuteronomy 33:4)

The Torah is an inheritance to us and is, therefore, part of our makeup. To not review it, would be to lead us away from our natural portrait. Without Torah, our life would be a misery. We often take upon ourselves only the parts of Torah that are convenient to us. The Torah wasn't just handed over; it was given to us as a commandment that we must fulfill.

"Open my eyes, so I may behold wondrous things from Your Torah." (Psalms 119:18)

The wonders of Torah are there even in its simple meaning. The problem is only that we close our eyes from seeing.

"If you seek it as silver, and search for it as for hidden treasures, then you shall... find the knowledge of HaShem." (Proverbs 2:4)

The scholars of previous generations didn't reach their prominent levels by quitting when a difficult question arose. It only inspired them to search harder.

"For they [words of Torah] are life to him who finds them, and healing to all his flesh." (Proverbs 4:22)

If you are feeling ill, learn Torah. Torah is medicine for the body and the soul. If you are feeling ill, first check to make sure you are using your time properly, making Torah study a priority. If you put it second when it should be first, you soul will become sick, causing your body to follow suit.

"But he who cleaves to HaShem your HaShem; he cries out and is immediately answered." (Devarim 4:4)

HaShem immediately answers those who learn Torah. Do not expect your prayers to be answered if you haven't made an effort to learn Torah that day.

"And it will be that before they call I will answer."
(Isaiah 65:24)

Even before they call to Him, HaShem answers those
who cleave to Him.

"It [Torah] is not in Heaven." (Deuteronomy 30:
12:13)

Do not assume that Torah study in this world is not
as precious as Torah study in the Heavenly Academy. The
Zohar says that each night, the *tzaddikim* and HaShem are
listening to our Torah study and finding pleasure from it.
Even the simplest Jew who learns Torah in this world is
breaking his entire being in order to do so. Even his simple
learning becomes very powerful.

"Its ways are pleasant ways, and all its paths are
peace." (Proverbs 3:17)

When a person's life is devoted to Torah, he finds
that even bitterness is made sweet.

"Do not turn aside from this thing that they tell you,
right or left." (Deuteronomy 17:11)

Isn't it enough to say not to turn away from the
Torah? Why does the Torah have to mention two directions?
This is because the ways of evil wear a disguise. When you
waver even slightly away from the Torah in one direction or
another, the evil inclination will overtake you. You will not
even realize you have strayed. Even if your ways are
righteous, you must still be careful that in your heart you are
thinking properly. Only through learning Torah and infusing
it into our lives can we be sure to stay levelheaded.

"I have given you a good teaching, my Torah; do not
forsake it." (Proverbs 4:2)

The Torah isn't just something you perform or read
about. It is something you must constantly review repeatedly,
otherwise, you are sure to forsake it.

"All desired effects cannot compare in value to it."
(Proverbs 8:11)

A person can desire many spiritual goals, but nothing can compare to the simple learning of Torah *l'shmah*, for its own sake.

"Its measure is longer than the earth and broader than the sea." (Job 11:9)

A person can't be rewarded in measure for his Torah learning because its power is beyond measure.

"Therefore, you shall teach them to your sons..."
(Deuteronomy 6:7)

The way to acquire Torah is to teach it to your sons and other Jewish people, who should be considered as your own sons. It is the actual handing down of the Torah to future generations that opens the Torah's light to a person.

"And you shall meditate on it day and night." (Joshua 1:8)

A person is not excused from learning Torah if he studied only during the day or night. This is a very common mistake by those who are busy during the day, at work, or in school.

CHAPTER 16:
EVIL INCLINATION

"Praiseworthy is the man who did not walk in the counsel of the wicked, and in the path of the sinful did not stand, and in the place of scorners did not sit. Rather the Torah of HaShem is his desire and in his Torah, he meditates day and night." (Psalms 1:1,2)

Why does it say, "Do not walk, do not stand and do not sit...?" Wouldn't it have been enough to say, "Do not stand with those not doing the will of HaShem"? The message we are being told here is, do not be naive and think that the ways of other nations won't affect you. Don't walk, stand, or sit as the other nations. Do not assimilate in any way, shape, or form - in order to look good in their eyes. Rather, occupy yourself with fulfilling HaShem's desire, and meditate on how to come close to Him through the Torah.

"You shall slaughter it of your own free will."
(Leviticus 19:5)
HaShem is telling us we should not think that He is going to destroy our evil inclination for us. We are the ones who must take the initiative to slaughter it, using our free will. HaShem has given us the tools to accomplish this challenging task.

"Woe to those who carve out engravings of sin."
(Isaiah 10:1)

One sin leads to the next and piles up to become an overwhelming burden. These very sins are etched upon one's bones. They become engraved in one's soul and being. The way to rectify them, Rebbe Nachman teaches, is to repent for the first sin of the bundle. All those that followed will naturally be rectified. If you cannot mend your sin or recall its details, say these passages of Psalms in the following order, as they have the ability to rectify the first sins of a bundle: 16, 32, 41, 42, 59, 77, 90, 105, 137, and 150.

"The path of the upright is to stay away from evil; he who guards his soul will preserve his way." (Psalms 16:17)
If we were guarding a treasure, certainly we would not travel to places where we could accidentally slip and break the treasure. We would stay away from robbers and bandits, not placing ourselves in their path. In the same way, we must guard our souls scrupulously as if we are caring for a valuable treasure. We should not take chances by taking roads we know might be slippery.

"Tremble and don't sin; reflect in your hearts upon your bed and be still *selah*." (Psalms 4:5)
Whenever you get into a confrontation with your evil inclination, awaken your good inclination. Reflect upon the final resting place given to man and quiet your passions. If you are patient, the thought will pass, and you will not sin.

"If your enemy is hungry feed him bread." (Proverbs 25:21)
Instead of fighting head to head, the smart one utilizes strategies to wear out his opponent. The Evil Inclination will not back away until you feed him something. Therefore, tell him you will feed him soon. Walk away from the sin and then feed him the bread of Torah until he flees.

"And do not go astray after your hearts and after your eyes." (Numbers 15:39)

Why does it say, "Do not stray after your heart" before it mentions the eyes? Don't we first see things and only then pursue the yearning in our heart to continue after the evil? The truth is that it isn't our eyes that lead us astray. If our heart were properly purified, we wouldn't even see things that we shouldn't.

"I made a covenant with my eyes not to gaze on a maiden." (Job 31:1)
Just as a person makes a covenant by circumcision, so must he make such a pact with his eyes not to gaze at anything improper.

"And against you is its desire, but you can prevail over it." (Genesis 4:7)
At times, the evil inclination arouses itself to such an extent that there seems no window through which to escape. Even during these times, you can succeed, if you truly want to. It may seem as an army rising up against you, but you can still prevail. The sword of your mouth can meet any uprising if you only arouse your heart and mind to pray to HaShem.

"Will a man draw forth fire into his lap and his clothes not burn? Will a man walk on coals and his feet not be scorched?" (Proverbs 6:27, 28)
The way of the evil one is to reason with a person saying, just taste a little and it won't hurt you. It's so obvious that you are going to get burnt from this evil action. So why are you doing it?

"For You are not a HaShem who desires evildoers; evil shall not dwell with You." (Psalms 5:4)
At the time of sin, we do not even consider the consequences of our actions. We are about to walk away from truth and give up a tremendous spiritual ascent, should we not overcome this temptation. HaShem certainly does not desire these actions, and we will be separating ourselves from

the bond with our Creator. This bond is our life force and the greatest asset we have; let us not lose it.

"Bruises and wounds purge away evil; so, do stripes, which reach the inward parts." (Proverbs 20:30)

Sometimes the only way a person can be purged of his evil transgressions is through physical suffering. It is often beneficial to endure the uncomfortable wounds, as this might help lead you on the right path once again. Emotional pain can feel even more painful than physical wounds. This too is very cleansing.

"Remember your Creator in the days of your youth, before the evil days come." (Ecclesiastes 12:1)

One should not say that when I am older, I will work on my evil inclination. Now is the time to overcome all negative traits, when they are burning inside at their fullest. If you wait, the flame will return later in life and you will not have the strength to extinguish the flames.

"If you do well, you shall be lifted up. If you do not do well, then sin will be crouching at the door; unto you will be its desire, but you may rule over it." (Genesis 4:7)

If you serve HaShem righteously then you will be drawn close and elevated. If you do not do HaShem's will, and let even one sin slip by, then the evil inclination will never let you find a moment of peace. Your desires to do wrong will increase until there is nothing left of you. Even in this low state, you may take control back and rule over your inclination once again - if you truly desire to do so. Many times, a person waits until he reaches rock bottom to pull himself up, but don't wait this long. It is a great rectification to stop oneself even in the middle of a sin.

"For you are dust and to dust shall you return." (Genesis 3:19)

If we are something made from dust, then how can we even think of sinning? Who are we to go after pleasures when we are literally nothing? Maybe that is the problem - we think we are something when we are not.

"Visit your neighbor sparingly." (Proverbs 25:17)
If your neighbor has a beautiful wife or daughter you find attractive, visit them sparingly. Should some of your peers' gossip about others, visit them less often. Only visit those whom you can lift up or those who will lift you. Don't visit for the sake of visiting, it leads to frivolity.

"HaShem tested Abraham." (Genesis 22:1)
We each think that we have been tested through and through by HaShem. We sometimes hear about sufferings of the *tzaddikim* in our generation, but we know very little of the suffering they truly endure.
When an army approaches a castle to overcome the king, the soldiers on the front lines endure the greatest tribulations of war. The same is true of the righteous of our generation, they are on the front lines and we are following behind. If not for their strong endurance ahead of us, we would not be able to bear the Satan's opposing forces.

"A master of his passions is better than a conqueror of a city." (Proverbs 16:32)
Today we think that money and power make someone great. Little do we realize that a truly great person is someone who possesses self-control. Very few have this, and few seek it as their true goal. What could be a greater victory than to overcome oneself?

CHAPTER 17:
REDEMPTION

"I will be like dew for Israel; it will blossom like a rose."(Hoshea 14:6)

Dew is a great gift from HaShem because it has only beneficial powers. HaShem will give us great sustenance and make us flourish.

"If not for HaShem, who was with us when men rose up against us?" (Psalms 124:2)
People always feel that their friends and family will support them in times of trouble, but in reality, HaShem is our only true unconditional friend, Who will never turn against us.

"And some of those of understanding shall fail to try them and purge and make them white until the time of the end because it is yet for a time appointed." (Daniel 11:35)
There have always been people who felt they could predict the redemption. They calculate and estimate, but their science is not truthful. They soon realize that they can't change HaShem's will with a calculator.

"If they merit [it], I will hasten it." (Isaiah 60:22)

We take the idea of *Moshiach's* coming for granted and assume it will happen overnight. It must be worked for and deserved.

"Behold, I will send you Elijah the prophet..." (Malachi 3:23)

Whenever any great king or prestigious person enters a room, they are announced so that those waiting can be prepared. Elijah is a crucial step in announcing the *Moshiach*, for us to make final preparations.

"If I forget you, Oh Jerusalem, let my right hand forget [its skill]." (Psalms 137:5)

If someone lost the use of his right hand, he would be helpless to do even simple tasks. Without Jerusalem, too, we are helpless and incapable of serving HaShem.

"Many of those who sleep in the dust shall awake, some to everlasting life and some to shame [and] everlasting contempt." (Daniel 12:2)

When all the deceased are resurrected they will get whatever they worked for when they were alive. When *Moshiach* comes, we will finally recognize our strength as the chosen of HaShem. If only we recognized it now, we would strengthen ourselves as a holy nation and bring the Redemption.

"Walk about Zion and encircle her; count her towers." (Psalms 48:13)

A person should always count the righteous people who are standing around him. When *Moshiach* comes, we will realize the good in one another. Every Jew is an entire world and a tower of *mitzvos*. Let us begin counting the merits of others; judging other Jews unfavorably delays the redemption.

"His splendor shall reign like [that of] a bridegroom." (Isaiah 61:10)

A groom has splendor because people are talking about him in a positive light. They search for his goodness and find it. HaShem's splendor is even more revealed and yet we fail to make him King.

"Then will our mouth be filled with laughter, and our tongue with song…" (Psalms 126:2)

We will laugh when the redemption comes since we will realize how easy it was to have brought it.

"They will make Me a sanctuary, [and] I will dwell among them." (Exodus 25:8)

Many kings want to be raised above their people, but not HaShem. He wants to "dwell with us" like a family member or a close friend.

"The moon shall be confounded, and the sun ashamed…" (Isaiah 24:23)

Those who lowered themselves and were humble, HaShem will raise them up. Those who were proud will be lowered. In a world of Truth (as we will have when *Moshiach* comes), a person can't raise his stature, or hide his greatness, as he could in the present world of confusion.

"You, 'Oh HaShem, are our Father, our Redeemer; Your Name is everlasting." (Isaiah 63:16)

It is mentioned many times in *Tanach*, that when the *Moshiach* comes HaShem's name will be everlasting. How is it not everlasting now? Something can't be everlasting if it is not appreciated deep within our hearts. We are so far from the true love of HaShem; a love that is everlasting.

"Rejoice with Yerushalayim, and be glad with her, all who love her…" (Isaiah 66:10)

Only those who love Jerusalem will be able to rejoice with her at the final redemption. All others will feel like party crashers.

"Be in pain, and labor to bring forth, 'Oh daughter of Zion, like a woman in labor, for now, you shall go out of the city, dwell in the field, [and] you come to Babylon; there you shall be rescued; there HaShem will redeem you from the hand of your enemies." (Michah 4:10)

A woman, who is in labor and then has her child, suddenly feels redeemed after the child is born. Her pain is stopped and joy reigns. Without the labor pains, there could be no birth.

"Behold, your king comes to you." (Zechariah 9:9)

How many kings want to come down from their stature in order to be with their subjects? As soon as we crown HaShem as our King, His palace will no longer be in the heavens, but the third Temple will descend from heaven to earth.

"I will no longer hide My face from them, for I have poured out My spirit upon the House of Israel." (Ezekiel 39:29)

There is the final and great redemption, and then there is the redemption of a person from his own darkness to light. When we return to HaShem, He, in turn, redeems us by revealing that which He had previously covered from us.

"The sound of weeping and the sound of howling will be no longer heard." (Isaiah 65:19)

We are so removed from a true love of each other, that we don't hear the cries of our fellow human beings. If we only listened, we would hear the true pains of exile. We would not be able to bear this and would elevate ourselves to such a level that even we could bring the final redemption.

CHAPTER 18:
NATURE

"The heavens speak of Hashem's glory, and the skies tell of His handiwork." (Psalms 19:2)

The heavens, which are comprised of the *Sefiros,* *melachim,* etc…show His infinite power. The physical version of the heavens shows His skill and creation.

"From the wings of the land we have heard song, glory to the righteous." (Isaiah 24:16)
It is known that each living organism cries out in its own praise of our Creator. The land calls out in praise of the righteous because it is the sages that rule over the physical world.

"I will also send the teeth of domesticated animals against them, with the venom of the creeping creatures of the dust." (Deuteronomy 32:24)
Nature was created simply for the reason of carrying out the will of HaShem. HaShem's agents are in all things, bringing glory to His name and helping the world to continue according to His plan.

"HaShem founded the land with wisdom; He established the heavens with understanding." (Proverbs 3:19)

You would think that the heavens would be formed with wisdom and the earth with understanding, as Kabbalah teaches us that wisdom is higher than understanding. The truth is that it took more work to create HaShem's light in a concealed manner, as it wanted to be revealed. After all, we were created by HaShem in order that He could share with us His light. The nature we see in this world is the highest light concealed in a lower form.

"More than the voices of many waters, than the mighty waves of the sea, HaShem on high is mighty." (Psalms 93:4)

Water has a tremendous amount of force and might. Most of the water in the world is continuously flowing non-stop from place to place. We can try and learn from watching the waves at a beach, to see the force and control HaShem has over the world. In but a moment water can sweep an entire ship or island into the sea, never to be found again. How much more can HaShem snap His finger and this world could vanish instantly.

"The sun, [when covered by] the moon, stood in its abode; they speed at the light of Your arrows, and the shining of Your glittering spear." (Habakkuk 3:11)

Light travels very quickly. It is interesting that a person who is blind is blessed to have stronger senses when it comes to other things. If only we appreciated the power of light, it would strengthen our spiritual abilities to see the light of HaShem. Unfortunately, instead it dulls our other senses.

"He made darkness His secret place; His pavilion around Him was dark with waters and thick clouds of the skies." (Psalms 18:12)

If HaShem was going to hide in darkness, why did He create all this light? Could it have been in order to blind us from seeing Him? The opposite; nature and light should strengthen our belief in Him.

"I shall be as the dew to Israel, he shall blossom as a rose, and he shall spread forth his roots as the Lebanon." (Hoshea 14:6)

It is dew that strengthens the ground and nurtures the plants. Just as dew falls every morning, so too, HaShem is bringing down spiritual dew from heaven every morning. All a person has to do is make a new beginning each morning and accept the coming day as an entirely new creation. Then he will blossom that day into a beautiful servant of Hashem, bringing gladness to those around him.

"Lift up your eyes upon high and perceive Who created these!" (Isaiah 40:26)

Whenever you see something physical, you should always lift up your eyes to HaShem and you will see the spiritual light of that object. HaShem surrounded us with nature so we could constantly have an opportunity to perceive Him through the physical world.

"The lion is the mightiest of animals and turns away before no one." (Proverbs 30:30)

We should be like the lion that puts no emphasis on physical fears. We should fear none other than HaShem.

"I shall consider HaShem to be in front of me at all times." (Psalms 16:8)

HaShem made us physical beings so to put Him in front of us in only a spiritual sense would be too difficult for us. We should relate to Him in a physical sense, like a peasant to a king, so we can feel true humility.

"Arouse yourself, oh north [wind], and come, oh south! Blow upon my garden, let its spices flow out; let my Beloved come to His garden and eat of its precious fruit." (Song of Songs 4:16)

Wind is an element that can be both gentle and harsh. We can learn from wind that being able to have a good balance of character is very important.

"The wolf shall dwell with the lamb, and the leopard shall lie down with the kid, and the young lion and the calf together... (Isaiah 11:6)

In the times of *Moshiach* there is such a level of peace that the animals will be gentle to one another. For now, though, we can learn a lesson from animals that being at war with others is inhuman.

"You, Oh HaShem poured a generous rain to strengthen Your heritage when it languished." (Psalms 68:10)

HaShem made nature such a large part of our life that it affects our daily activities immensely. If something affects a person so much, shouldn't he learn about it and try to understand its wisdom and reasoning?

"Then shall the trees of the forest sing out at the presence of HaShem because He comes to judge the earth." (I Chronicles 16:33)

Why should the trees sing when HaShem judges us? The trees have been around for a very long time. They live longer than any other living organism, so they have seen all of history. And as it says, "*eitz chaim hee*," the trees will surely give for us a favorable testimony.

"When I behold the heavens, the work of Your fingers, the moon and the stars which You established; what is man, that You are mindful of him?" (Psalms 8:4-5)

This shows the great mercy of HaShem because compared to the celestial powers we are nothing, and yet HaShem still hears our cries and sustains us.

"I lift my eyes up to the mountains; where shall my help come from?" (Psalms 121:1)

We should look to the mountains for encouragement, as we can see that even the smallest of them was uplifted. HaShem will also help even the smallest and simplest of us.

"The voice of HaShem is upon the waters, the HaShem of glory thunders, HaShem is upon many waters." (Psalms 29:3)

HaShem is speaking to us through the waters. He is saying, "move, move!"

Glossary

Achdus- Togetherness
Ahavas Yisrael- Love of one's fellow Jew
Al naharos Bavel- Prayer said about the Destruction of the Temple
Aliyah to the Holy Land- Immigrating to Israel
Am haaretz- Common Jewish Man, sometimes referring to someone unlearned in Jewish laws
Am Yisrael- Jewish Nation
Amen- Used after a prayer, or other formal statement to express solemn ratification or agreement
Amidah- See definition of Shmoneh Esrey
Amora- Their legal discussions and debates were eventually codified in the Gemara. The *Amoraim* followed the *Tannaim* in the sequence of ancient Jewish scholars.
Aron Kodesh- The **Torah ark** or ark in a synagogue
Aseres hadibros- The Ten Commandments
Atik- Ancient
Aveirah / Aveiros- Sin / Sins
Avodah- Service
Avodas Hashem- Service to G-D
Avos- Forefathers
Avrechim- Married men who learn in Kollel
Ba'al koreh- The individual who chants Torah from the scroll at the synagogue
Bar-mitzvah- A ceremony and celebration for a Jewish boy at the age of 13 when he takes on the religious duties and responsibilities
Bedikas chametz- Checking for unleavened bread before Passover
Begashmius- Material benefits from this world
Beis din- Jewish Court
Beis Din shel Maalah- Court in Heaven
Beis Hamidrash / Beis Medrash- House of Study, Synagogue
Bekitsche- Decorative coat worn on Shabbos by chassidish men
Ben- Son
Benched- Blessed
Beruchnius- Spiritual benefits
Birkas hamazon- Blessings after eating bread
Bitachon- Faith
Blatt- Pages of Talmud
Bnei Yisroel- Children of Israel
Bochor / Bochorim- Young Single Man/Men
Borchu- Blessing said during the Marriv prayer recited by the Chazan
Boruch Hashem- Thank Hashem
Bracha- Blessing
Bracha Shehakol- Blessing over eating food

Bris milah / Brisim- Circumcision
Chachom- Wise man
Chalav Yisrael- Cow milked by a Jew
Chalukah- Traditionally the first hair-cut of a boy at age 3
Chas v' shalom- It shouldn't happen
Chassan- Bridegroom
Chassid- Follower or person seeking higher purity
Chassuna- Wedding
Chatzos- Midday or Midnight
Chavrusa- Study partner
Chazal- Sages
Chazzan- Prayer Leader
Cheder- Religious school for boys
Chevrah Kaddisha- The local burial society
Chiddushei Torah- Original *Torah* insights
Chidushim- New thoughts in Torah
Chochmah- Wisdom
Cholent- Hot Meat dish traditionally served for Shabbos Lunch
Chovos halevavos- A Main work in Jewish literature, **Duties of the Heart** by
Rabeinu Bachya ibn Paquda zt'l
Chumash- Five books of Moses
Churban- Destruction (of the Temple)
Cohen / Cohanim- Priest
Daven / Davened- Pray, Prayed
Dayan- Judge
Der heiliker- The Holy Man
Divrei Torah- Words of Torah
Drush- Homiletic interpretation of the Torah
D'vekus- Closeness to G-D
Eibershter- G-D in Yiddish
Ein K'Elokeinu- There is None like Our G-d
Eliyahu Hanavi- Elijah the Prophet
Emunah- Faith
Eretz Yisrael- Holy Land (of Israel)
Erev- Evening before Shabbos or a Holiday
Farbrengen- Feast made by Chassidim
Gabbai- Aramaic) (a) the person responsible for the proper functioning of a
synagogue or communal body (b) an official of the Rebbe's court, who admits
people for yechidus, private meetings
Galil- Northern Israel
Gan Eden- Garden of Eden
Gaon- Great Rabbinical Scholar
Gemara- Talmud
Gematria- Numerical value
Gemilus Chassadim- Kindness to others
Geonim- Great Sages
Gilgul- Reincarnation
Goy / Goyim / Goyishe- Non-Jew (s)
Hagba'ah- The ceremony of lifting the Torah

Haggadah- Text read on Passover
Halacha- Jewish Law
Har Sinai- Mountain where the Jews received the Torah
Hareini Mekabel- I accept upon myself
Hashem- G-D
Hashgacha Pratis- Everything comes from Hashem; personal supervision
Haskama- Approbation
Havdalah- Prayer to conclude the Shabbos
Heichalos- The heavenly mansion
Hiddur Mitzvah- "The beautification of a *mitzvah*," actions that glorify, or beautify, the observances and celebrations within Jewish tradition
Hillula- Memorial
Im Yirtze Hashem- With the help of G-D
Kaddish- Recited for the deceased Soul
Kadoshim- Holy Sacrifice
Kallah- Bride
Kameyos- Amulets
Kapara- Forgiveness
Kavanah- Concentration, intent. The frame of mind required for prayer or performance of a mitzvah (commandment)
Kavod Hatorah- Respect for the Torah or Sage
Kavod- Respect
Kazayis- is a Talmudic unit of volume approximately equal to the size of an average olive.
Kedusha- Holiness
Keili- Vessel
Kerias Hatorah- Reciting the Torah in a Minyan of 10 Men
Ketuvim- Writings
Kever- Grave
Kiddush- Blessing recited on Shabbos over a cup of wine
Kiddush Levana- Blessing over the New Moon recited Monthly
Klal Yisrael- The Jewish Nation
Klal Yisroel- Jewish Nation
Kohanim- Priests
Kohen Gadol- Head Priest
Korbanos- Sacrifices
Krias Shema- Recital of the Shema
Ksav Yad- Personal handwriting
Lag b'Omer- A Jewish holiday celebrated on the 33rd day of the Counting of the Omer celebrating the end of Rabbi Akiva's students dying. It is also the memorial of Rebbe Shimon Bar Yochai.
L'Chayim- A word used to express good wishes just before drinking an alcoholic drink
L'chovod Shabbos Kodesh- In honor of the holy Shabbos
Le'illui Nishmas- For the sake of the deceased
Levi- 1) A descendant of the tribe of Levi, which was set aside to perform certain duties in connection with the Temple; 2) Son of Jacob (Israel). Ancestor of the tribe of Levi.
L'shem shamayim- For the sake of Hashem alone

Ma'aseh Merkavah- Works of the Chariot
Machlokes- Controversy
Madrega- Level where a person is holding in spirituality
Maggid- Story teller / Sometimes referring to R. Dov Ber Mezritch, Leader of Chassidus after the Baal Shem Tov
Malach / Malochim- Angel (s)
Mamash- Enthusiastic response: WOW
Manna- The food that fell from the sky to feed the wandering Israelites in the Bible
Marror- Bitter Herb used on Passover
Marshal- Parable
Mashpia- Spiritual guide
Mashul- "comparison" or "parable"
Mechuten- Son's father-in-law
Melachim- Angels
Melamdim / Melamed- Teachers/teacher
Mezuzah- A scroll placed on doorposts of Jewish homes, containing a section from the Torah and often enclosed in a decorative case
Midbar- Desert
Midos- Character Traits
Midrash- Referring to the exposition, or exegesis, of a biblical text
Mikveh- Ritual Bath house
Minchah- Afternoon prayer service
Minyan- Quorum of 10 men during the prayer service
Mishnah / Mishnayos- The first compilation of the oral law, authored by Rabbi Yehudah HaNasi; the germinal statements of law elucidated by the Gemara
Misnagedim- Opposers
Mitzvos- Commandments
Mizbeiach- The Altar in the Temple
Mizrach- East, designates the direction in which we should pray (from our vantage point, towards Jerusalem.
Moshe Rabbeinu- Moses, Greatest prophet who ever lived.
Moshiach- *The anointed one*, who will herald in a new era for Judaism and all humankind.
Motzei- Night after Shabbos or Yom Tov
Mussar- The study of character correction
Nachas- Pride or gratification, especially at the achievements of one's children
Neshamah- Soul
Nevi'im- Prophets
Niggun / Niggunim- Melody (s)
Nigleh- The revealed aspects of the Torah
Nishmas- Nishmas Kol Chai, the breath of every living thing) is a Jewish prayer that is recited following the Song of the Sea
Olam Haba- The World to Come
Pardes- The "Heavenly Orchard"
Parnasa- Income
Parsha- Weekly Portion read from the Torah on Shabbos
Parshios- Parchments
Pasul- Unfit

Perush- Commentary
Pesach- Holiday of Passover
Peyos- Sidelocks
Pidyon / Pidyon Nefesh- Redemption for the soul, in form of a note and money given to a Sage
Pilpul- Loosely meaning "sharp analysis"; refers to a method of studying the Talmud through intense textual analysis in attempts to either explain conceptual differences between various halakhic rulings or to reconcile any apparent contradictions presented from various readings of different texts.
Posuk / Posukim- Verse, Verses
Pshat- Simplest meaning, based on the text and context
Rabbanim- Sages
Rachmonus- Mercy
Raphael- The angel of healing
Rav- Rabbi who answers halacha questions
Rebbetzyn- The Rabbi's Wife
Remez- Meaning "hint" in reference to scriptural interpretations
Ribono Shel Olam- Master of the World / Hashem
Rishonim- The leading rabbis and poskim who lived approximately during the 11th to 15th centuries, in the era before the writing of the Shulchan Aruch, and following the Geonim.
Rosh Chodesh Seuda- Festive Meal for the new Jewish month
Rosh Hashanah- Jewish New Year
Rosh Hayeshiva- Head Rabbi of a Yeshivah
Ruach Hakodesh- Divine Inspiration
Ruchniyus'dike- Spiritual connection to something
Schlepp / Schlepping- Drag around
Schmooze / Schmoozing- Talking and hanging out
Sechel- Understanding
Sefer / Seforim- Book (s)
Sefiros- 10 attributes/emanations in Kabbalah
Segula- Remedy or charm
Seraphim- Angels
Seuda- Festive meal
Shaaloh- Question for a Rav to avoid stumbling on another occasion
Sha'atnez- The prohibition against wearing clothes woven of wool and flax.
Shabbos- The Jewish Sabbath, a day of rest and spiritual enrichment.
Shabbosdiker Kapota- Shabbos garment
Shacharis- Morning daily prayer service
Shalosh Seudos- Third festive meal on Shabbos
Shamash / Shammes- Lit. servant. 1) The candle that is used to light other Chanukah candles; 2) the janitor or caretaker of a synagogue
Shamayim- Heaven
Shas Bavli and Yerushalmi- Bavli Talmud compiled in Bavel, Jerusalem Talmud compiled in Jerusalem before the Bavli Talmud
Shas- Complete order of the entire Talmud
Shavuos- Holiday commemorating the giving of the Torah
Shechinah- The Divine Presence
Shechitah- Slaughter of kosher animals

Sheker- Falsehood
Shemoneh Esreh- The central prayer of the Jewish liturgy
Shidduch- Dating through a matchmaker
Shikker- Plastered (drunk) in Yiddish
Shir Hama'alos- Song of Ascents in the Psalms
Shiras HaShirim- A Song written by King Solomon
Shiur- Torah class
Shliach- Messenger
Shochtim- Slaughterers of kosher animals
Shtiblach- Small synagogues
Shtreimel- Fur hat worn during Shabbos
Shul- Synagogue
Shulchan Aruch- Code of Jewish Law
Siddur- Prayer book
Simcha- Joy and celebration
Simchas Torah- Holiday Celebrating the Torah
Sippurei Tzaddikim- Stories of righteous people
Siyum- Party for finishing a Torah book
Sod- Secret of the Torah
Sukkos / Succah- Jewish Holiday celebrated in booths
Tallis- Prayer Shawl
Talmid- Student
Talmud Chachom- Wise student
Tanach- Acronym of Torah (Law), Nevi'im (Prophets) and Ketuvim (Writings).
Tanna- Jewish sages whose views were recorded in the Mishnah in the first and second centuries
Tefila / Tefilos- Prayer(s)
Tefillin- Holy Scriptures wrapped in a box with leather straps to attach to the head and arm
Tehillim- Psalms
Teshuva- Repentance
Tikkun- Repairing
Tikun Chatzos- (lit. "Midnight service"); a prayer recited by pious Jews at midnight, lamenting the destruction of the Holy Temple
Tishah b' Av- Memorial Day to recall the destruction of the Temple
Toiveled- Purified oneself in the Mikvah
Tzaddik / Tzaddkim- Lit. Righteous person(s). A completely righteous person often believed to have special, mystical power.
Tzaddik Nistar- Hidden righteous man
Tzedakah- Charity
Tzetl- Note
Yechidus- Personal time spent with one's rebbe
Yeshiva- School for learning Torah for older boys or men
Yeshuah- Redemption
Yetzer Hara- Evil inclination
Yichus- Family Background
Yid /Yiddala / Yidden – Jew (s) in Yiddish
Yiddishkeit- Yiddish for Judaism
Yiras Shamayim- Fear of G-D

Yom Tov- Holiday
Yungeleit / Yungerman- Yiddish for young man
Zechus- Merit
Zeide- Grandfather
Zemanim- Times of the day

Made in the USA
Coppell, TX
21 December 2020

46812203R00066